LASER LIGHT

by Herman Schneider
illustrated by Radu Vero

McGraw-Hill Book Company

NEW YORK   ST. LOUIS   SAN FRANCISCO

AUCKLAND   BOGOTÁ   DÜSSELDORF   JOHANNESBURG

LONDON   MADRID   MEXICO   MONTREAL

NEW DEHLI   PANAMA   PARIS   SÃO PAULO

SINGAPORE   SYDNEY   TOKYO   TORONTO

Library of Congress Cataloging in Publication Data

Schneider, Herman, date.
  Laser light

  Includes index.
  SUMMARY: Discusses laser and non-laser light, the laser beam and
apparatus used to produce it, and the applications of lasers. Includes
experiments.
  1. Lasers—Juvenile   literature.   [1. Lasers. 2. Experiments] I.
Vero, Radu. II. Title.
  TA1682.S36   621.36′6   77-26620
  ISBN 0-07-055451-X

23456789 BPBP 83210

ACKNOWLEDGMENTS

The author wishes to thank the following people
for their valuable suggestions:

Mr. Henry Berman, former Director of the
Scientific Instrument Division, Carl Zeiss-Jena,
U.S.A.

Mr. Leo Schneider, Senior Science Editor,
The New Book of Knowledge Encyclopedia

Dr. Edward A. Spiegel, Professor of Astronomy,
Columbia University, New York,
and formerly Professor of Physics,
New York University

CONTENTS

LASER
LIGHT

INTRODUCTION

THE NEAREST THING TO MAGIC WANDS

It's easy to think of lasers as magic wands. Some lasers actually look like wands. All lasers do things that seem like feats of magic. Look at some examples:

- Aim a laser at a steel razor blade. Press a button and . . . pop! A beam of laser light punches a hole in the steel blade.

- Aim the laser beam at a sheet of printed paper. The beam burns off the printing, leaving the paper untouched.

- Aim the beam at one of these balloon-inside-a-balloon combinations. The *inside* balloon explodes while the *outside* balloon is unaffected.

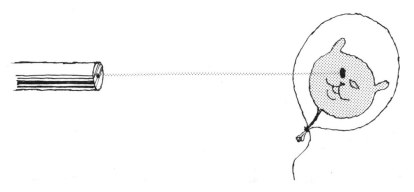

But these are just stunts. What *useful* jobs can a laser do? Thousands. A few examples:

- *A surgeon* aims a laser beam at an ugly, dangerous skin tumor on a patient's face. In a few minutes, without pain, and without loss of blood, the tumor is burned away, leaving no scars. (See page 81).
- *An astronomer* aims a laser beam at the moon. With an instrument called an interferometer (page 99), the astronomer measures the earth-moon distance with an accuracy of 20 centimeters.
- *A machinist* points a laser beam at a wheel to be used in an airplane gyro compass. While the wheel is spinning a thousand times a second, the beam finds any uneven spots on the wheel, and trims them away. The wheel is left perfectly balanced. (See page 88.)

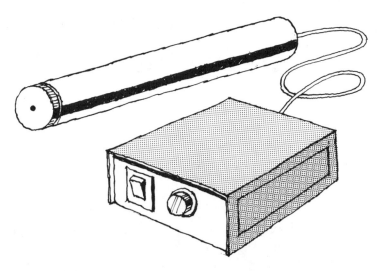

What is the laser *beam* that does these amazing things?
What is the laser *apparatus* that produces such a beam?

A laser beam is light: a special kind of light.

A laser apparatus is an electric lamp: a special kind that produces laser light.

Before we find out about lasers, we need to find out about ordinary, non-laser light. Then we can see how laser light is different in some ways but similar in others.

1 SOURCES OF ORDINARY LIGHT

If you're reading this book by daylight, you're making use of the most common source of light—the sun. That's also true on a cloudy day, or indoors by reflected daylight. Even if you're reading by moonlight, you're using sunlight reflected from the surface of the moon.

At night you probably read by electric light. But you might be getting light from a candle, oil lamp, or campfire. In some places in the Far East, you might even see by the light of several dozen fireflies glowing in a little cage!

That's certainly a wide variety of different *sources*. Yet they all produce the same *effect*: light.

There are two groups of light sources: (1) those that produce light from heat (thermal) and (2) those that produce light in other ways (luminescent).

Thermal Sources—Flames and Wires

When you rub your hands together briskly, you can feel the heat produced against friction. Remember the sensation of sliding down a rope or a pole: the greater friction, the more heat. Still greater friction? . . . look at a grindstone in action, sharpening a steel knife. Those sparks are

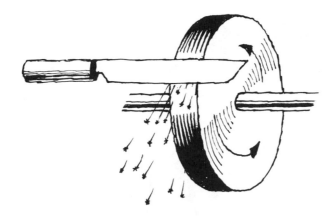

bits of steel, glowing in the extreme heat produced by friction of the knife against the grindstone.

A shower of sparks from a grindstone is not a very convenient reading light. But you have used a similar device: a candle. The light of a candle comes from trillions of glowing sparks of carbon. The heat comes, not from friction, but from burning.

Most candles are made of paraffin, a compound of carbon and hydrogen. When you put a lighted match to a candlewick, you melt a bit of paraffin in the wick. The melted paraffin turns to vapor and catches fire. The hydrogen in paraffin burns easily, with plenty of heat—but very little light. The carbon doesn't burn as easily. First it heats up and glows, and then it burns. The light of a candle flame comes mainly from the glow of burning bits of carbon, heated by burning hydrogen.

You can collect and examine the carbon from a candle flame. You will need a candle in a holder, and a white porcelain dish. (The dish will not be damaged.)

Light the candle and hold the dish at the tip of the flame for a second or two. You'll get a small black disk of carbon.

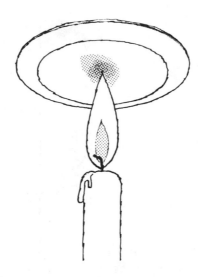

Wipe it off, then try again a little further down on the flame. Then still further. You'll get a series of rings, like this:

A candle flame is hollow. Inside the flame, paraffin vapor flows out from the wick. The flame itself is glowing carbon, heated by burning hydrogen and by its own burning.

Almost all flame sources of light work in the same way. Glowing carbon emits the light in a kerosene lamp, a bonfire, an oil lantern, or a pine-knot torch.

The glow of carbon is yellowish white. Other substances

glow with different colors. Sprinkle a few grains of table salt on a flame; the color is deeper yellow. Borax or boric acid will give a green glow. In a burning log, other substances give flashes of red, purple and orange.

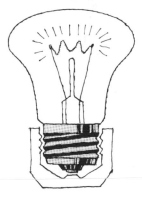

The glow of an electric bulb also comes from heat. An

electric current causes a thin tungsten wire to heat up and emit light.

You can produce the same effect by holding a thin strand of picture wire across the terminals of a battery.

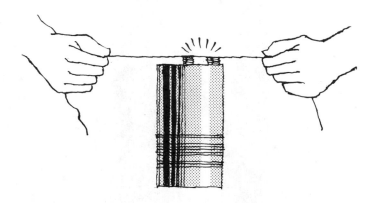

The picture wire and the tungsten wire in a bulb really produce light in two steps: (1) The electric current heats the wire. (2) The heated wire emits light.

When you accidentally touch a lit 100-watt bulb, you're almost ready to say that it's not an electric light but an electric heater. And that's almost entirely true; the bulb emits about 2 percent light and 98 percent heat. (On your electric bill you're charged for the whole 100 percent, of course.)

Isn't there a better electric lamp, one that gives more light and less heat for the money? To find it, we have to give up the thermal two-step system: (1) electricity to heat, (2) heat to light, and go to:

Luminescent Sources—Tubes and Fireflies

In a luminescent light source, nothing has to be heated to produce light. The most common example is a fluorescent

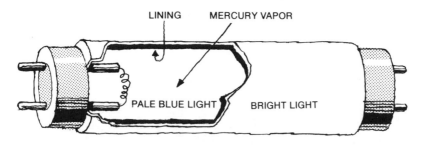

tube. Such a tube works by a different kind of two-step system, like this:

(1) Electricity produces an almost invisible pale blue light.
(2) This almost invisible light is changed to a bright visible light.

The diagram shows the interior of a fluorescent tube. The tube is filled with a gas, mercury vapor. Electric current causes the vapor to glow with a faint blue light. The light strikes the lining of the tube. The lining is similar to the inside coating in front of a TV tube. It emits a strong light. (A small amount of heat is also produced, but much less than in a tungsten bulb.) The color of the light depends on which substance has been used to line the fluorescent tube.

There are many other luminescent sources of light. Neon signs, argon lamps and sodium-vapor street lights are similar to fluorescent tubes. All of them give more light and less heat than tungsten bulbs. They feel warm, not hot, to the touch. They are more efficient than tungsten bulbs.

A *still* more efficient lamp should feel even less warm— in fact, cool. And it does, as you found out if you picked up a cool glowworm or firefly. A glowworm is the larva, and a firefly is the adult form of a family of beetles called Lampyridae (notice the "Lamp").

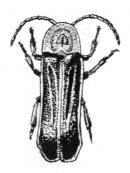

These efficient living lamps emit light by a chemical process. They have glands that make a chemical compound called *luciferin* (from the Latin for "light-maker"). When luciferin is combined with oxygen (oxidized) it emits a greenish glow. Another gland makes an oxidizing chemical, *luciferase.* When the glowworm or firefly feels a need to glow, it releases a bit of luciferase. This oxidizes a bit of luciferin and a flash of light is emitted.

Light comes from living things; light comes from fluorescent tubes and tungsten bulbs and flames; from thermal sources and from luminescent sources; all kinds of light in all colors and brightnesses; ordinary light and the very special kind called laser light. To understand them, we first have to explore the basic question:

What Is Light?

Suppose the answer to this question were "Nobody knows." That might discourage you from reading further. A better answer is "Nobody *quite* knows." Scientists know, or almost know, a great deal about light. As to what they don't quite know, you'll judge that for yourself as you read further.

The Particle Theory

"Light consists of tiny luminous particles" was one theory. According to the English scientist, Sir Isaac Newton (1642–1727), these particles are emitted by the sun, by flames and by all sources of light. The particles strike against objects and bounce off—they are reflected. When the reflected particles from an object strike your eye, you see the object.

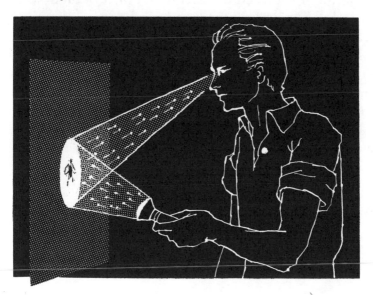

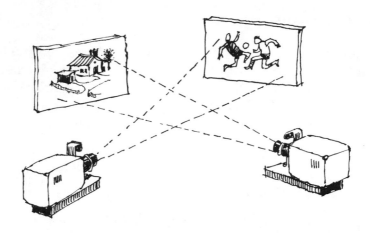

Here's an experiment that might be used to test the particle theory. Two slide projectors, each with a picture slide in it, are pointed at two screens. Projector *A* is turned on, forming a picture on Screen *A*. Then it is turned off. Projector *B* is turned on, forming a picture on Screen *B*. Then *both* projectors are turned on at once, so that the two beams cross each other.

If light consists of a stream of particles, what might happen? Won't the two streams of particles bump against each other? Won't the two pictures be distorted in some way? If you can borrow two projectors and screens, try it.

It doesn't happen. Both pictures are clear, undisturbed. Such an experiment might seem to finish off the particle theory.

The Wave Theory

What other theory is there about light? "Light consists of waves," said the Dutch scientist Christian Huygens (1629–

1695). These might be something like ocean waves or sound waves. Ocean waves travel through water; sound waves travel through air and other substances. Light waves travel through . . . what?

You might guess (and people did) that light travels through air. But then they found that air is a rather thin blanket around the earth. How do sunlight and starlight travel millions of miles through empty space to us?

A theory was constructed: There is an invisible, perfectly transparent, weightless gas, the *ether*, that fills all space in the entire universe. (This ether has nothing to do with the ether gas used by doctors.)

"A light source, such as the sun or a fire, causes the ether to vibrate and make waves. These waves travel swiftly through the ether. When the waves from a light source, or from an object that reflects light strike your eyes, you see the object."

The ether theory seemed reasonable—especially if the ether could be proven to exist. How do you prove the existence of something that is transparent, invisible and weightless?

The Michelson–Morley Experiment

In 1881, two scientists named Michelson and Morley set up an experiment to find out whether the ether exists. This experiment requires some mathematical calculations. However, you can get a rough idea of the experiment by first thinking about a strange boat race.

A ship is standing still in a calm, quiet body of water. Four fast motorboats, and their drivers, are in the water next to the ship. One boat is at the bow, facing forward;

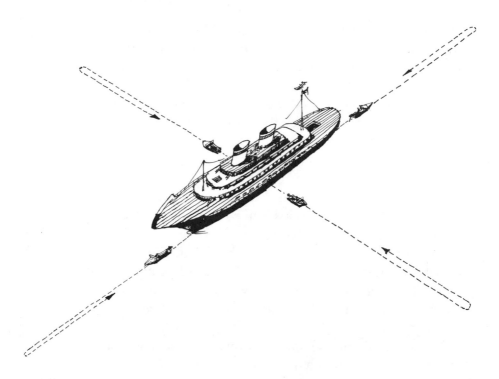

one is at the stern, facing backward; the other two are at the sides, facing away from the ship.

At a signal, each boat drives away from the ship at full speed (all four boats at the same speed). One minute later the next signal is given. All four boats turn around and head back for the ship at full speed. Obviously they will reach the ship at the same moment.

Now the experiment is repeated, but with one difference. As the starting signal is given, the large ship also begins to move very *slowly*, forward. *Now* will the four boats return and reach the ship at the same time?

No, because the ship has moved forward through the water. This forward motion has shortened the distance for the front boat and lengthened the distance for the rear boat. It hasn't changed the distance for the side boats. It just changed the place where they bump the slowly moving ship.

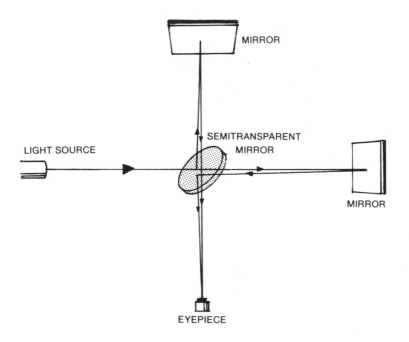

Here is a diagram (much simplified) of the Michelson–Morley apparatus. The "ship" is an electric light. The four "boats" are four beams from the electric light, shining forward, backward and sideward. The beams are "turned around" by mirrors. The "calm water" is the ether—if it exists. The "movement" of the ship is the actual movement of our earth as it revolves around the sun.

If the ether exists, the whole apparatus is moving through it, like the ship through the water. If so, the four beams should not return together. The forward beam should arrive first, the sideways beams next and the rearward beam last.

And what were the actual results? All four beams arrived exactly together! More precise apparatus was constructed and the experiment repeated . . . with the same results. No ether—and therefore no ether waves as an explanation of how light travels.

Waves—Or Particles?

Shall we go back and accept the particle theory? Not yet. An English scientist, Thomas Young (1773–1829) performed an experiment with light and screens, which is a bit complicated. You can perform a simpler experiment with an umbrella.

At night, open a black cloth umbrella and look through it at a street lamp. If light consists of particles, they should come through the spaces between the threads of the cloth. You should see lots of little bright spots, in a regular pattern.

Instead, you will see something like this. Strange, crisscross patterns appear. These are called *interference patterns*, and they can only be caused by waves.

You have seen interference patterns in water. When water waves strike the piles of a dock, they break up into smaller waves that roll sideways and interfere with each other. (See page 18.) Light waves (believe in them for a moment) when they strike the threads and spaces of the cloth umbrella, break up into crisscrossing waves that form an interference pattern.

Let's take one more look at the wave-or-particle problem. Let's look at the problem through Polaroid sunglasses. You will need two pairs, or one pair that has broken so

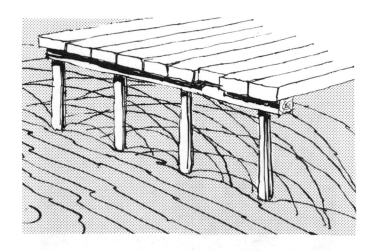

that you have two separate lenses. (Polaroid lenses had not been invented when Newton, Huygens and Young did their experiments.)

Before doing the experiment, look at the pair of chairs at the top of page 19. Imagine that light consists of *particles*, like tiny bullets. You can aim a gun at the spaces in the first chair; if you aim right, the bullets will pass through the spaces in the second chair, right through to the target.

If you lay one of the chairs on its side, you can still aim so as to send your bullets through to the target.

Suppose light consists of *waves*. Tie a length of clothes-line through both chairs. (See page 20.) Make up-and-down waves. They pass through both chairs. Then lay one chair sideways. Try to make waves; no success. They are stopped by the second chair.

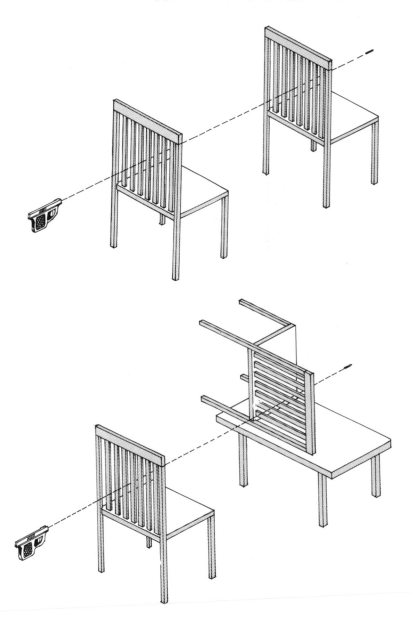

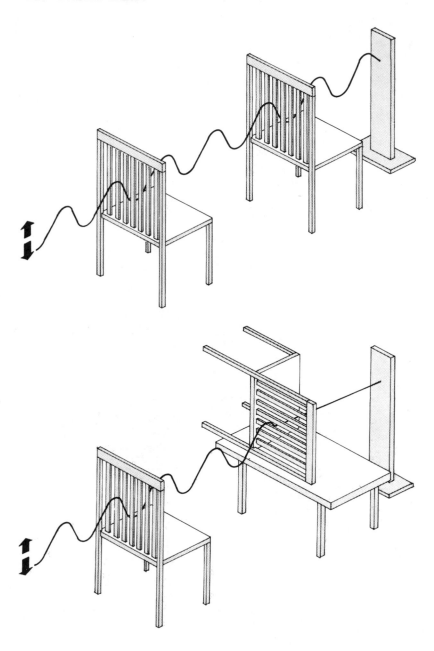

Now, instead of bullets and clotheslines and chairs, let's do the experiment with light and Polaroid lenses. These lenses have tiny crystals in parallel rows, like the parallel spaces in the chairs.

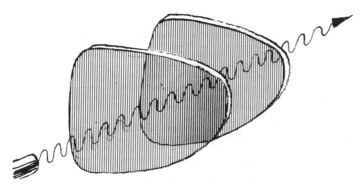

Hold the two lenses one in front of the other, like this. This is like two chairs, both upright. You can see through the two lenses. You can shine a flashlight through them. This could happen with light-as-particles or light-as-waves.

Now turn one of the lenses sideways. This is like laying

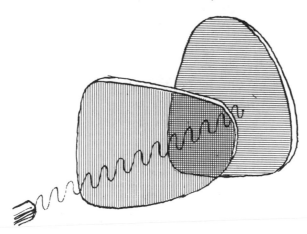

one of the chairs sideways. Can you see through the lenses? Can you shine a light through them? You can't. *Only* the wave theory can easily explain such a result!

Something more to think about: You caused the clothes-line to shake up and down, or *oscillate.* These up-and-down oscillations were able to pass through the up-and-down slats of the chairs. If you had made sideward oscillations, or slanting ones, they would have been stopped.

But most light consists of oscillations in every direction: up and down, sideways, slanting. When you shined a flashlight through the first Polaroid lens, only the up-and-down oscillations got through. We say the lens *polarized* the light. This polarized light could pass through the second lens, *if* the second lens was in the same position as the first. When you turned one lens, the polarized light was stopped.

Or Wavicles?

So, do we accept the wave theory of light? We have these arguments in its favor:

(1) Light can be polarized, as shown by the Polaroid experiment.
(2) Light can form interference patterns, as shown by the umbrella-and-light experiment.

But we have one important piece of evidence *against* the wave theory of light: the Michelson–Morley experiment. This experiment proved that there is no ether, no substance in which light waves are formed. We can talk about waves-in-water, waves-in-air—how can we talk about waves-in-nothing?

The particle theory requires no ether. Shall we accept the particle theory? Then how do we explain polarization and interference patterns? Something had to give way.

What gave way was the "either-or" idea: *either* particles *or* waves. In 1905, Albert Einstein (1879–1955) suggested that light is *both!* He offered calculations to show that light consists of particles traveling in a wave form. (In fact, they are sometimes called wavicles.)

Think of somebody riding on a carousel horse that moves up and down. The person could be compared to a *particle* traveling within a *wave* form. Something like that can be said about light; that it consists of particles moving within a wave form. In some experiments the particle idea shows through; in others, the wave idea.

Photons

Light particle-waves are called *photons,* from the Greek word for "light." A *photo*graph is a picture made by light. The "on" in photon means a particle. Electr*on*, neutr*on* and prot*on*: all are particles in atoms.

A 100-watt bulb sends out about 10 trillion photons per second; a small flashlight, about 100 billion per second; a glowworm, about 100 million per second.

Photons are particles of light with properties:

(1) They are extremely small, with comparative-ly great space between them. If you could enlarge a photon to the size of a grain of salt,

then the space between two photons would be about 1,000 meters. (Does that give us a hint as to why the two projector beams didn't seem to interfere with each other?)

(2) This is especially hard to believe: Photons exist *only when they are moving.* They move at the speed of light—because they *are* light. Through space this speed is about 300,000 kilometers (186,000 miles) per second. There is no such thing as a stationary photon.

Then what happens to a photon if you try to stop it? Any of these things can happen:

(1) *Transmission.* Shine a flashlight beam through a pane of glass. Photons from the flashlight hit the glass, slow down slightly, pass through the glass and pick up their former speed, in the same direction. Transmission is one of the things that can happen to photons.

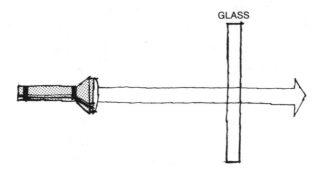

GLASS

(2) *Refraction.* Shine the flashlight through a curved piece of glass, such as an eyeglass lens or magnifying glass. Again the photons hit the glass, slow down and then resume their speed. But this time their path is bent, or *refracted.* Refraction is another thing that can happen to photons.

LENS

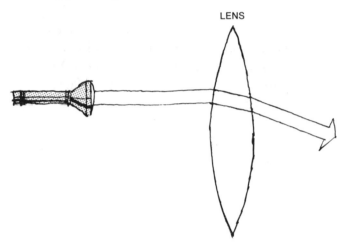

(3) *Reflection.* Shine the flashlight slantingly at a mirror. Find its spot of light on the wall. Photons from the flashlight strike the mir-

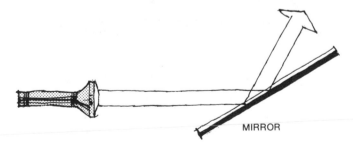

MIRROR

ror, bounce off at the same speed and strike the wall. The mirror *reflects* the photons to the wall, and then the wall reflects the photons into your eyes. Reflection is another thing that can happen to photons.

(4) *Transformation.* Shut your eyes and face the sun. The sun's photons are hitting your face. Feel your skin get warm. Some of the photons, striking your face, vanish as particles. Their energy is transformed into heat energy in your skin. Transformation can happen to photons, and so can transmission, reflection and refraction.

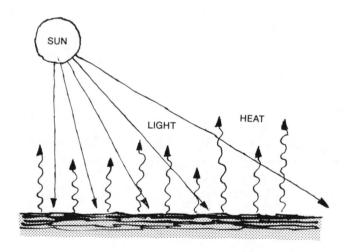

Why are there differences? What makes mirrors reflect while plain glass transmits or refracts? Why does sunlight cause a dark pavement to heat up more (transform more photons) than light-colored pavement? The answers to these questions have to do with the wave nature of light.

2 THE WAVE-NESS OF LIGHT AND OTHER THINGS

All Kinds of Oscillations

The waves you are most familiar with are water waves, because you can see them. They have a regular repeating motion. That's the basic thing about all waves—water waves, sound waves, light waves and radio waves. All of them have a regular repeating motion called *oscillation*. High to low, or forward to backward, or side to side—they oscillate.

The world is a very oscillatory place. You can *see* a clock pendulum oscillating. You can *hear* the oscillations made by a violin string. You can *feel* the oscillations of the flow of blood in your pulse. You can *plan* a birthday party by the oscillation of the earth traveling in an ellipse around the sun. One oscillation takes one year.

Planets revolving, fiddles playing, clocks ticking—all are forms of oscillation. You can't measure or count the speedy ones, such as strings vibrating, or the much speedier ones in light waves. But you can study the slower ones, such as pendulums swinging. From these slower ones you can get an idea of what happens to the swift ones.

Periods and Frequencies

Here's a pendulum made of a thread and an eraser. If the thread is about one meter long, the pendulum's swing will take about one second. Shorten the thread and you shorten the length of time it takes the pendulum to swing back and forth. This length of time is called the *period*. Long pendulum thread: long period. Short thread: short period. To put it another way, the shorter the pendulum, the more frequently it swings—it has a higher *frequency*. A longer pendulum oscillates at a lower frequency.

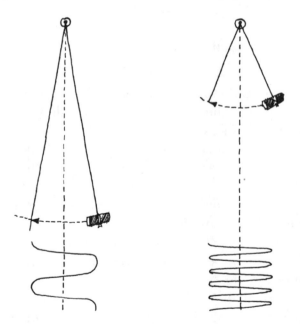

A pendulum can take another form of oscillation: around and around, in an ellipse or in a circle. Try it; you'll find that the same rules apply. Long string: low frequency; short string: high frequency.

Now let's think about some oscillators with very short "strings." Every atom consists of a central part, the nucleus, surrounded by oscillating electrons. Atoms are extremely tiny. The ink in this dot · consists of about 50 billion (50,000,000,000) atoms. The electrons in these atoms have a frequency of about 100 billion revolutions per second.

These numbers are not being given to amaze you. They have a definite relationship to why an egg yolk is yellow, why water is transparent and how a laser beam can destroy a skin tumor without harming the flesh underneath. Later. First we need to explore another important aspect of wave-ness:

Reinforcement and Resonance

Listen to the sound of a seashell held lightly against your ear. Some people believe it's the sound of the sea, preserved in the seashell. A pleasant idea, but you can get the same effect with an empty tumbler or soup can. Try it with various sizes. Each size container gives a sound of different pitch.

The container doesn't make the sound. The air around the container is already full of many faint sounds of different pitch. All those sounds are oscillations of the air. There are the sounds of outside traffic, of little breezes, of the refrigerator and other household machinery, even the sound of blood circulating in your ears. When you hold a seashell or other hollow container against your ear, one of these sounds is favored, or *reinforced.*

But which sound? The one whose frequency—oscillations per second—matches the size of the container.

That is, an oscillation enters the open end; races down to the closed end and bounces back; and reaches the open end again just as the next oscillation is about to enter. The two oscillations travel down and back together, and then the next one comes along, and the next; adding up, getting louder until you hear sounds that would be too faint to hear without reinforcement.

Short containers reinforce sounds of high frequency; long containers, low frequency. If you had a container whose length could be changed, you could choose different frequencies to reinforce. A sliding bottom could do the trick, as with this gadget.

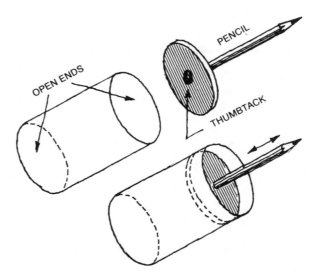

As you slide the movable bottom, you change the length of the air space in the container. Each length matches the frequency of one sound out of all the different sounds in the air. This matching of frequencies is called *resonance*, from the Latin for "sound again." As you create different lengths of air space, it resonates to different pitches of sound *received*.

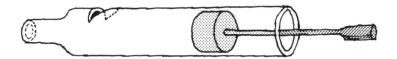

Now look at a reverse example. This little whistle *emits* sounds of different pitch, according to the length of the air space in the whistle. The length can be changed by sliding a little plunger in or out. Exactly the same principle works for a trombone, whose full name is slide trombone. Sliding a tube in or out changes the length and therefore the frequency of the emitted sound. Long tube, low frequency; short tube, high frequency.

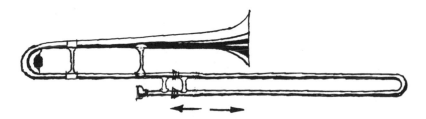

This method of changing frequency by changing size is used in many devices. For example, when you turn your radio dial to 83, you change the size of a part (the variable condenser) so that it resonates to radio waves whose frequency is *830*,000 oscillations per second. The same thing happens in the channel selector of your television receiver. And the same thing happens in a *tunable laser*. Turning a knob changes the frequency of the emitted laser beam. We can pick the frequency that destroys the ink on a page, but leaves the paper unharmed—or vice versa!

Now we're almost ready to enter the invisible place, the interior of the atom. In here is generated the photon-waves, or wave-photons, or wavicles, by which you see, or take pictures, or get tanned or sunburnt—or punch holes in steel.

3 INSIDE THE ATOM

Exploring by Resonance

The interior of the atom is an extraordinary place, of unbelievable tininess (50 billion atoms in this dot ·) and unbelievable speed (electrons revolve around the nucleus at about 100 billion times per second).

Actually, we can't look inside or measure or count, in the ordinary sense. But scientists have found some extraordinary ways. For example, see how much can be done by using the principle of resonance.

Here are four pendulums hung on one tightly stretched string (you can use steel nuts or pebbles). Set pendulum *A*

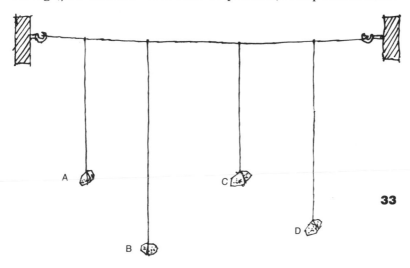

swinging and see what happens . . . pendulum *C* begins to swing. It resonates to pendulum *A*, because it has the same length, and therefore the same frequency. The other pendulums, with different frequencies, merely jiggle a bit, but without vigor. They are not in resonance with pendulum *A*.

Now consider this arrangement. There's a pendulum inside the box, swinging constantly. The pendulum's frequency is unknown, and you can't open the box to find out. But there's another pendulum outside, with a string whose length you can change.

Try any length. Set the pendulum swinging and see what happens. Does it just jiggle a bit or does it take on a

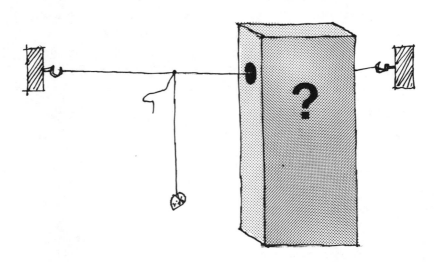

full rhythmic swing? If it just jiggles, try another length, and another. When you get a healthy swing, the two pendulums are in resonance. Count the frequency of the outside pendulum and you'll know the frequency of the one in the box.

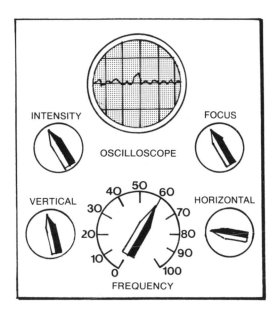

The box with its contents is like an atom. The inside pendulum is like an electron oscillating around a nucleus. The outside pendulum is like an electric oscillator whose frequency can be regulated. When the oscillator's frequency is not in resonance with the electron's, we see a weak jiggly line on an instrument called an oscilloscope. When the two frequencies are in resonance, we see a strong peak as shown on the next page.

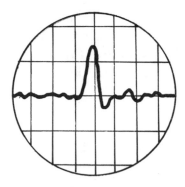

Now, with a very very rough idea of how it's done, let's "look" inside an atom to see what goes on.

The Rutherford Atom

We'll begin with the simplest atom, an ordinary atom of hydrogen. This is the *H* in H_2O, water. It's made of a nucleus consisting of one proton, with an electron revolving around it and rotating (spinning).

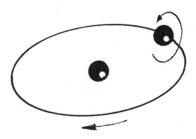

Such an atom, as shown in this diagram, is called a Rutherford model. It was named after the English scientist, Ernest Rutherford (1871–1937). In 1911 Rutherford first described atoms as tiny solar systems, with the nucleus as the "sun" and with electrons revolving and rotating like tiny "planets."

The Rutherford model has been enormously useful in exploring the nature of matter and energy. However, it has one drawback—it doesn't exist. Atoms are not tiny solar systems, but in some ways they behave as if they were.

Then what is the true structure of the atom? Nobody quite knows. But that doesn't mean that scientists have to stop their research until they get the answer. Think of the box with the unknown pendulum inside. Think of how we can determine its frequency without opening the box.

But there may not be a pendulum inside the box! There may be an oscillator of another kind. It may be a balance wheel of a watch ticking back and forth. It may be a vibrating steel spring, oscillating up and down. All kinds of things can oscillate in resonance with the outside pendulum. We can assume it's a pendulum in the box unless we come upon evidence that it's something else. In the meantime,

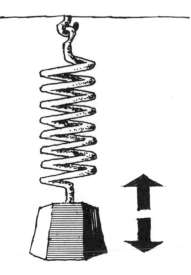

we can stay with the Rutherford model of the atom. It's a simple model, and it gives us something to work with.

Notice the plus mark for the proton. This indicates a *positive* electrical charge. A proton is positively charged. An electron, marked minus, has a *negative* charge. The minus doesn't mean that an electron is lacking a charge, but that it is oppositely charged from a proton.

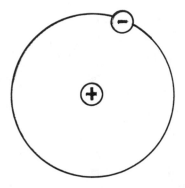

Protons and electrons attract each other. This attraction keeps the electron from flying out of the atom. At the same time, the electron's motion keeps it from being drawn into the nucleus by the pull of the proton. In balance between the two, the electron stays in its tiny orbit.

This is the ordinary situation for a hydrogen atom. The electron is said to be in the *ground state*. (Other atoms have more electrons, each with its own ground state. But we'll stay with the hydrogen atom because it is the simplest, with the fewest parts.)

Up from the Ground

Electrons can be forced out of the ground state. They can be forced farther out, against the inward pull of the proton nucleus. But it takes energy to do this. The energy can come from several sources. Among these are:

(1) Heat energy. Hold an iron nail in a flame. Heat causes electrons in the iron atoms to move out of the ground state.
(2) Light energy. Shine a light at a photo exposure meter; you force electrons of selenium atoms or cadmium atoms out of their ground state.
(3) Electrical energy. Send an electric current through a fluorescent tube. You force electrons of mercury atoms out of their ground state.

Where do the electrons go, after they leave the ground state? They move farther out, into another orbit around the nucleus. There are several orbits; four are shown here. The first is the ground state (G). The others are called *excited states* (E).

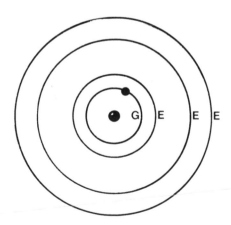

To which excited state does an electron go? That depends. Kick a football with plenty of energy and it goes far. Kick it with less energy and it doesn't go quite as far. An electron can be kicked out of the ground state into any of the excited states; which one depends on the energy in the kick. A 2,000-degree flame will kick an electron into a higher state than a 1,000-degree flame.

However, notice that there are several *distinct* orbits, or excited states. For example, there's an excited state 2 and excited state 3, but there's no $2^1/_2$ or $2^1/_4$.

The Quantum Theory

It takes a certain exact quantity of energy, called a *quantum*, to force an electron out of ground state into state 2. A certain different quantum will send it from ground to state 4. An electron in state 2 can be kicked up to state

4—by a quantum that is exactly the difference between those two quanta.

It's somewhat like climbing a ladder. A certain amount of energy will take you from rung 1 to rung 2. But no amount of energy will take you to rung 1½, because there's no rung there.

ALL ENERGY COMES IN EXACT PACKAGES, QUANTA

There are no fractions of quanta. There are no fractional excited states.

This theory, that energy comes in exact, distinct quanta, was first worked out by the German scientist Max Planck (1858–1947).

The quantum theory isn't easy to accept. Nothing in your daily life seems to support it. If you kick a football 32 meters, won't a tiny bit less kick send it 31.99 meters? If a gas flame heats an iron bar to 287°C., won't a bit higher flame heat it to 287.3°C.? If your car is buzzing along at 55 mph., won't a tap on the gas pedal send it to 55.17 mph.?

Yes: the answer is yes to all these questions. But these are questions about *large amounts* of energy: to move a football, to heat an iron bar and to propel a car. These large amounts, however, are really the sum total of quadrillions of small energy packages—quanta—within molecules, atoms and parts of atoms. Within these tiny particles there are no fractions, only whole quanta.

There we are with electrons in excited states. Each one was kicked up there by a quantum of energy. But they don't just sit there, excited and waiting. They immediately fall back to a lower state. Each one, as it falls, gives back the quantum of energy that raised it to the excited state.

An electron in state 2, dropping back to ground, returns a certain quantum of energy. An electron in state 4 dropping to ground state returns a larger amount. Or an electron may drop from state 4 to 3, emitting a quantum, and then drop the rest of the way to ground, emitting a different quantum.

What are these emitted quanta of energy? Here comes a staggering idea: *Energy quanta are photons!* You are reading this page by daylight or artificial light. Either way, the light begins in atoms where electrons are kicked into excited states by some form of energy—heat, electricity, chemical energy, and so forth. The excited electrons drop back to lower states and emit photons. The photons race out at full speed, 300,000 kilometers per second, until they strike something. Some of them are striking this page and are reflecting into your eyes.

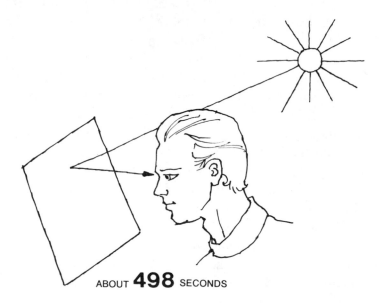

ABOUT **498** SECONDS

If you're reading by daylight, the photon's trip from the sun to this page took about 498 seconds. By artificial light, if the lamp is 1 meter away, the photons reached you in about 3 billionths of a second.

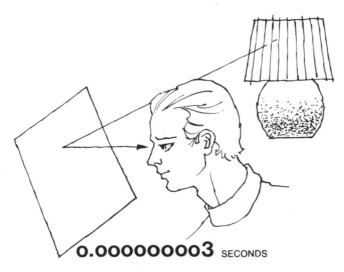

0.000000003 SECONDS

Bright Light and Dim Light

All light travels at the same speed, but not all light is the same. For instance, if you move the page closer to the lamp, the light on the page will be brighter. That's because you're catching more of the photons being emitted by the

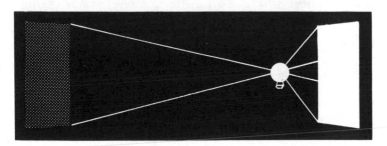

bulb. And, therefore, fewer photons are reaching other places in the room. These deprived places are called shadows.

Another way of getting more light on the page is to replace the bulb with a higher-wattage bulb—a 100-watt instead of a 50-watt, for example. The 100-watt bulb uses twice as much electricity and delivers more than twice as many photons.

More photons per second = brighter light
Fewer photons per second = dimmer light.

The Colors of Light

The color of sunlight is different from the color of your lamplight, which is different from the color of a neon sign, which is different from . . . and so forth. How are the different colors of light related to photons? The difference is in the energy carried by the photons.

A lot of energy is needed to kick an electron from ground state to state 4. When it falls back it emits a high-energy photon. From ground to state 2 or state 3 takes less energy, and the return produces a lower-energy photon.

How do these photons of different energy show their colors? By the waves that accompany the photons. A high-energy photon is accompanied by high-frequency waves—many oscillations per second. Lower energy photons: lower-frequency waves. The *different colors of light* consist of *different frequencies.*

This diagram bears the names of different colors of

visible light. The numbers refer to the frequencies of the light waves that produce these colors.

The colors go from red to orange to yellow to green to blue to violet. The numbers go from 4×10^{14} to 8×10^{14}. The 10^{14} means that 14 zeros should be added to the number.

4×10^{14} 5×10^{14} 6×10^{14} 7×10^{14} 8×10^{14}

RED   ORANGE   YELLOW   GREEN   BLUE   VIOLET

For example, 5×10^{14} can be shown in a longer way as 5 followed by 14 zeros (500,000,000,000,000), or 500 trillion oscillations (cycles) per second. Find that number on the graph and you'll see that it is in the range of orange light with a touch of yellow in it. Light with a frequency of 6×10^{14} would have a blue color.

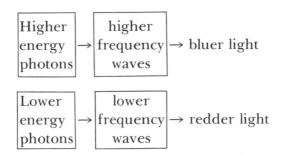

Higher energy photons	→	higher frequency waves	→ bluer light
Lower energy photons	→	lower frequency waves	→ redder light

A mixture of all the colors, in the proper proportions produces white light.

Infrared Light

Look on page 45 at the left end of the chart, before the red. Another way of saying "before the red" is *infrared*. You can't see infrared light, even though it exists. But you can feel it. Hold your hand close to, but not touching, your forehead. Feel the warmth.

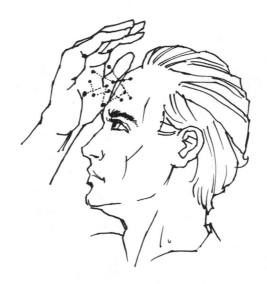

Photons emitted by your hand are striking your forehead. Photons from your forehead are striking your hand. These are all low-energy photons, not strong enough to produce visible light; but they produce heat as they bounce back and forth. The photons were emitted by electrons that had been kicked up and dropped back only a short way, in the atoms of your warm skin.

Now use your hand to open the refrigerator. Reach in for a snack. Your hand is still emitting low-energy photons; they strike the cold interior of the refrigerator (the air and the walls). *But the cold interior is also emitting photons.* These have a lower energy than your photons. The result of this energy exchange is that you lose. You give away more energy than you receive; therefore you feel colder.

Absolute Zero

There's a bottom limit to this trading of photons. Atoms or molecules that have no heat at all emit no photons at all. This occurs at *absolute zero*, which is minus 273.26° on the Celsius scale, or minus 459.69° Fahrenheit.

At any temperature above absolute zero, photons are emitted—even in a wild howling snowstorm in Antarctica. They are low-energy, low-frequency photons, but real— just as real as the photons in the brilliant colors of fireworks.

Ultraviolet Light and Beyond

Look at the right end of the chart, beyond the violet. The Latin for "beyond" is *ultra*. *Ultraviolet* light is produced by high-energy photons accompanied by high-frequency waves. The ultraviolet part of sunlight causes sunburn and tanning of your skin. A photon of ultraviolet light carries about 10,000 times the energy of an infrared photon.

Still higher energy photons, with very high frequencies, are *X rays*. These contain such high energy that they can pass easily through skin and muscle tissue—but not as easily through bone. This difference makes it possible to photograph the skeleton and tissue of the body.

Gamma rays are photons of still higher energy and wave frequency. Usually they are produced, not by oscillating electrons but by oscillations in the nucleii of certain atoms.

Still higher, perhaps the highest of all, are *cosmic rays*. These are atomic particles emitted by the sun and other stars. Cosmic rays are about 1,000 times as powerful as X rays. Fortunately for us, most cosmic rays, when they reach our atmosphere, collide with air particles and scatter some of their energy. Otherwise this planet would not be a fit place for man or beast—or tree or bug, for that matter.

Incoherent Light

Let's take one more look at ordinary light, before we look at the extraordinary light called laser light.

Your desk lamp emits ordinary light. Turn on the switch and an electric current (a stream of electrons) crowds its way through the thin tungsten filament of the bulb. The crowding throws atoms of tungsten into violent helter-skelter oscillation—that is, they become hot. The oscillation kicks electrons of the tungsten atoms to higher energy states. They immediately drop back, emitting photons. Over and over again, each electron moves from lower to higher states and back again, emitting photons, millions of times a second.

These emitted photons are not all alike, because the motions of the atoms that emit them are not all alike. The "heat motion" (called thermal motion) of atom *A* is not exactly equal to atom *B* or *C* or *D*. Therefore the energy in the emitted photons is not the same. *And the waves are not the same.* Their frequencies are different because frequency is related to the energy in the photon. Their timing is different because atom *A* may be beginning an oscillation at the moment when atom *B* is in the middle of one.

Therefore, the light coming out of an electric bulb, and practically all other light, is composed of a jumble of frequencies, out of step with each other. This jumbled light is called out-of-phase, or *incoherent* light (from the Latin for "not stick together").

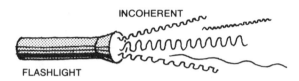

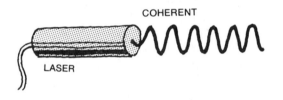

Now let's imagine a lamp that produces light waves of *exactly* the same frequency, all *exactly* in phase. Let's see how such light would be different from ordinary, incoherent light: (1) Of course it would have a different name: coherent light. (2) It would have a vastly different effect: it would be a beam of laser light. Let's find out more.

THE COHERENT LIGHT OF LASERS

Coherence to the Rescue

Imagine this situation. It's necessary to break down a large, heavy wooden door. Perhaps it's the door of a castle, with a fair maiden imprisoned inside, and a brave knight and soldiers outside. The knight could command his soldiers to beat at the door with wooden clubs. Each soldier is slightly different from the others, each beats with his own strength, at his own rate (frequency), in or out of phase with the others. It becomes an incoherent attack, with no results except a lot of clatter.

Let's try a different attack. Assemble all the clubs into one large club—a battering ram. Assemble the soldiers around it so they can ram at the door with their united strength—all at the same frequency, in phase. Result: a rescued maiden, thanks to a coherent attack.

Coherent light comes out of a laser apparatus. Later you will find out some details about how the apparatus works and how laser light is used. Right now you might like to speculate a bit as to how such light can be put to work. You would be in the same situation as scientists of about thirty years ago, when coherent light was first being explored.

50

What could they do with light that has these characteristics:

(1) Coherent light *can be concentrated* into a very small space. (And light can be converted to heat.) How can we use a very small source of very high temperature energy?

(2) Waves of coherent light are absolutely *uniformly spaced*—far more uniformly than the spaces on the most perfect meter stick. How can we use coherent light as a measuring device?

(3) These absolutely uniform waves are made by the absolutely *uniform oscillations* of electrons in atoms. Can we use such oscillations as time counters, more accurately than ordinary clocks?

(4) Coherent light can *carry messages*, the same as telephone cables or radio waves. A coherent beam as wide as a hair can carry several thousand telephone messages at the same time. Can we replace telephone cables with beams of coherent light?

There are hundreds of other such questions. Some have been researched and answered successfully; others not. Later we'll find out about the uses of coherent light from lasers. First let's find out how laser light is made.

Photons as Energy Traders

In the previous chapter, you reached into the refrigerator for a snack. As you did so, you traded photons from your hand with photons from the refrigerator. You gave out photons of higher energy than you took in. Therefore, you came out the loser, and your hand became colder.

This kind of photon trade, back and forth, sometimes with profit, sometimes with loss, takes place all the time, everywhere in the universe. Atoms that are not at absolute zero are busy trading photons for others of higher, lower or equal value. Even atoms at absolute zero (very few of those around) when struck by a photon, gain a bit of energy. Therefore they are able to go into action, emitting weak photons.

These photon trades are not simple cases of "I'll give you this and you give me that." There are several distinct types of photon trades. All are involved in producing laser light. Before we examine these trades, let's look at some symbols of the traders.

- This hollow circle is a symbol for an atom in a low-energy state. (Any atom consists of a nucleus surrounded by one or more orbiting electrons.) In this atom, shown by a hollow circle, the electrons are mostly or all in the ground state. Therefore the atom is a low-energy atom.

- This filled-in circle shows an atom in the excited state. The fill-in is energy. The nucleus is the same, but some or all of the electrons have been boosted to higher states.

- This is a photon. The head is shaped differently, to indicate that a photon is a different kind of particle. The wavy tail indicates that the photon is accompanied by waves, as are all photons.

Now let's look at the photon exchanges that are taking place between your hand and the refrigerator, as well as everywhere else in the universe. There are three types.

TYPE 1. SPONTANEOUS EMISSION

Many of the atoms in your warm hand are in the excited state (*A*). Their electrons drop back to lower levels, and each emits a photon (*B*). The photon hits the wall. This process is *spontaneous*; it isn't set off (stimulated) by outside particles. It happens because of the atom's own excited-state energy.

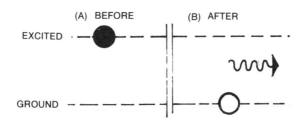

Spontaneous emission may, or may not, happen in one atom at the same time as in its neighboring atom, or in trillions of nearby atoms. So the waves from spontaneous emission are disorganized and incoherent with each other.

TYPE 2. ABSORPTION

Photons emitted by your warm hand strike the low-energy atoms of the refrigerator walls (*A*). They boost these atoms to higher energy levels. *The photons disappear!* Their energy is *absorbed* in boosting electrons to higher states (*B*).

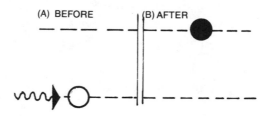

Absorption doesn't happen to *any* photon striking *any* atom. Each photon carries its own exact quantum of energy. Each atom has its own exact built-in set of energy levels. When quantum and level match each other, absorption takes place. Otherwise, no trade; the photon keeps going.

TYPE 3. STIMULATED EMISSION

The initial letters of these two words are the *s* and *e* of la*s*er. We won't take up the other letters at this time, because your hand is still in the refrigerator. Your hand is producing photons by *spontaneous emission* (Type 1) and giving them off into the refrigerator. That's why your hand is getting colder and colder.

Many of the photons emitted by your hand are being *absorbed* by the low-energy atoms in the cold refrigerator walls (Type 2). But, here and there in the walls there happen to be some atoms *already* in the excited state. This may be because (1) they have already received some photons from you or (2) because in the helter-skelter photon trade among atoms, they have already received some photons and haven't had time to return them.

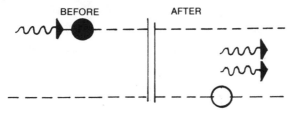

Two strange things happen to an excited atom when it receives a photon of the right quantum: (1) The atom *drops* to a lower energy level! (2) The atom emits a second photon together with the first! This second photon has waves of exactly the same frequency as the stimulating photon. And both are exactly in phase—crest to crest. Therefore, the two sets of waves are coherent.

That's what we were looking for: coherent light. This light, or *radiation*, is produced when an incoming photon *stimulates the emission* of two outgoing photons. So there you have the *s-e-r* of la*ser*: *s*timulated *e*mission of *r*adiation.

Now for the *l-a* in *l*aser. *One* photon went in; *two* came out. This doubling gives us *light amplification*. So we've spelled out the whole word *laser*: *l*ight *a*mplification by *s*timulated *e*mission of *r*adiation. This process was first noticed and described in 1916 by Albert Einstein.

We've spelled the word, but do we have a laser? No, because ordinary stimulated emission is just hit-and-miss, here and there among the atoms. It's like giving two clubs to some of the soldiers and letting them wallop randomly at the gate, along with the one-club soldiers.

Photons Strike Together

To make stimulated emission useful, it needs to be organized and controlled. The knight needs to order his soldiers to (1) line up, (2) join forces and weapons and (3) strike together. These three steps take place in a laser. Before we examine them, let's release your hand, rapidly cooling off in the refrigerator.

In the cold refrigerator air, most of the atoms are at low level. That is, most of their electrons are in the state of lowest energy: the ground state.

Let's assume that there are four possible energy levels: ground (low-level), excited-1, excited-2, excited-3. Although most of the electrons are low-level, a few are at excited-1, a very few at excited-2, and perhaps a very *very* few at excited-3.

Atomic Populations

A graph of this population of atoms would look like the diagram on top of page 57. (This is a graph of *average* conditions. Actually, the electrons are constantly hopping up and down the energy levels.)

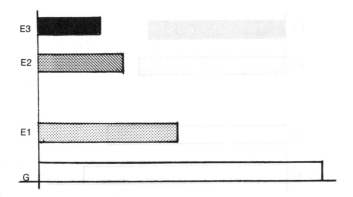

Your hand is warmer than the refrigerator air. See below how its population of atoms is distributed. The majority are still low-level, but not as many as in the cold air. An increasing number are at the excited levels. (Excited-level atoms are capable of stimulated emission, the *s-e* of laser.)

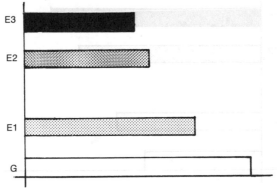

Consider something warmer: your hand close to a hot radiator. (See top of page 58.) A further increase in the higher-level atoms; a further decrease in the low-level atoms. Raise the temperature still further; the trend in

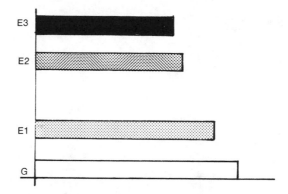

population change continues. BUT, no matter how much you raise the temperature, the atom population is always distributed like the above: at ground level, most; at excited-1, fewer; at excited-2, still fewer; at excited-3, fewest. There are never more at 3 than at 2 or 1 or ground.

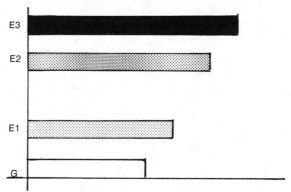

Population Inversions

Suppose for a moment that we *could* work up a population like the above: more excited-3 atoms than ground-level atoms. This is called a population *inversion*. Look at the opportunities:

Let's say there are five times as many excited-3 atoms as in a normal collection of atoms.

5 · This means there are *five times* as many possibilities of spontaneous emission (Type 1) of photons.

5×5 · Each of the emitted photons has *five times* the chance of colliding with an excited atom. This is because there are five times as many excited atoms to collide with.

5×5×2 · Each such collision produces, by *stimulated emission* (Type 3), two photons with coherent, in-phase waves.

5×5×2×2 · These two photons can collide with two excited atoms. Each collision produces a doubling by stimulated emission.

And again and again and again . . . hundreds of doublings, all in a billionth of a second (called a *nanosecond*). A sudden mighty shower of photons; a tremendous smash of energy.

At last have we achieved true coherent waves, a true laser action?

No, not quite. Look at those hundreds of doubling steps. The photons in all those steps were not emitted at exactly the same moment. They were emitted pair *after* pair. The time interval between one doubling and the next is very small—perhaps a thousandth of a nanosecond. But it means that the waves carried by the photons are *not* all in step, *not* coherent.

So, we have armed each soldier with many clubs instead of only one. We have shown the soldiers how to strike the gate at *almost* the same moment.

Almost is not good enough. It won't break down the door.

5

INSIDE LASERS

Getting Ready for Lasers

To break down the door, to achieve a true laser action, we have to solve two problems:

(1) How to produce a population inversion. (Unless we can, we won't have that mighty shower of almost-in-phase photons.) Then, if that problem is solved:

(2) How to store those photons, while we change them from almost-in-phase into truly-in-phase.

These were the problems that Dr. Charles H. Townes set out to solve. Together with several other scientists, he found the solutions. In 1954, he demonstrated the first working maser.

No, that's not a misprint. *Maser*, not *Laser*. The *M* stands for *Microwave*. *Microwave Amplification by Stimulated Emission of Radiation*. Dr. Townes experimented with microwaves. Their frequency is only about one ten-thousandth as much as light waves. And so is the energy they carry, which made them easier to experiment with.

The first lasers were developed in 1957 by Dr. G. Gould and in 1958 by Dr. C. H. Townes and Dr. A. L. Schawlow.

The first maser was not very powerful. It couldn't punch a hole in anything, or do any other of the "almost magic" jobs described on page 1. But it served a useful purpose nevertheless. It was the "ticker," the timekeeping mechanism for the most accurate clock ever built up to that time. It was accurate to one second in about 1,000 years. (Today's best clocks? One second in about 30,000 years!)

Inside an Ammonia Clock

Since the maser was part of an *ammonia* clock, let's talk about ammonia first.

Ammonia gas has the formula NH_3. One molecule of ammonia consists of one atom of nitrogen joined to three atoms of hydrogen. The atoms are attached to each other in the form of a little four-sided pyramid, like this. (There

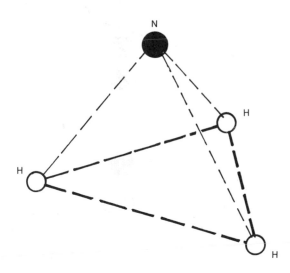

are no lines in the molecule; they are just drawn to help you see the pyramidal form.)

The atoms in an ammonia molecule, like all atoms, are in constant oscillation. This oscillation is done mainly by the nitrogen atom. It moves from the top of the pyramid, down through the base to the other side (making an upside down pyramid) and back to the top. This oscillation takes place approximately 23,870,000,000 times per second (rounding out the last six places). Changes in temperature or pressure have no effect on this rate of oscillation. So the oscillation of nitrogen in ammonia can be used as a time divider. It can tick off time like the hairspring of a watch. Most watches tick five times per second. An ammonia molecule ticks almost 24 thousand million times per second.

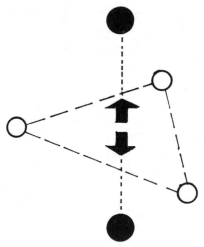

Back to the ammonia maser, the time-ticking part of an ammonia clock. Here's a diagram of the principal parts.

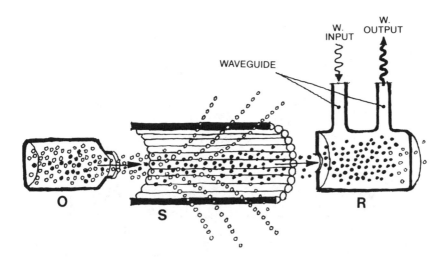

(O) The Oven. Ammonia gas flows into this oven. It is heated under high pressure, causing many molecules to go into the excited state. (That is, their *atoms* go into an excited state, but the oscillation within the pyramids remains unchanged.) The ammonia molecules, some excited and some in the ground state, flow through a nozzle into:

(S) The Separator. This is a chamber surrounded by electrically charged bars. The electric charge attracts the ground-state molecules; the excited molecules are not affected. They keep going straight ahead into:

(R) The Resonant Cavity. Consider the population of this cavity. It consists of a great many excited ammonia molecules and very few unexcited ones. This is the inverse of the usual situation. (See page 58). *We have achieved a population inversion.* That's Step 1 of the maser (or laser) action.

Step 2, the amplification effect, follows immediately:

(1) *Spontaneous emission* takes place in a few excited molecules. Each emission produces one photon.

(2) These photons strike other excited molecules and *stimulate* them. Each stimulated molecule emits a second photon, in phase with the photon that first struck the molecule. This is a doubling process.

(3) Double after double after double, the photons build up in swift landslide, a sort of chain reaction, in a nanosecond, producing huge quantities of photons. These photons were all emitted by the ammonia molecules, so they all have the same frequency. However, they were not all emitted at the same moment, so they are not in step, not in phase, not coherent. But there they are, bouncing around inside the resonant cavity.

Resonant cavity—remember the seashell? It resonates to sounds of a certain frequency, and reinforces them. Which sounds? Depends upon the size of the seashell.

The same thing happens in the resonant cavity of the maser. The size is exactly right to resonate to the frequency of ammonia molecules. As the photons bounce around wildly in the cavity, resonance forces them into step, into coherence. (The soldiers are tying their clubs together and falling into line.) When the photons (and their waves) are completely in phase, coherent, they are let out to do battle.

Not much of a battle, though, for this early ammonia maser. The lined-up photons were let out through a wave guide to control a clock mechanism. The frequency was so exact that the clock kept time with an accuracy of a second in about a thousand years.

In an ammonia clock, the maser's job was to produce exactly timed waves. The maser was working mainly as an oscillator.

Most often, however, masers or lasers are used as *amplifiers.*

Amplifiers

The process of amplification is especially useful to astronomers and other scientists involved with space.

You too are involved with space, in a manner of speaking. A radio station's waves travel through space into your radio receiver. The radio waves are converted into sound. If the waves are powerful, you get a loud sound. If the waves are weak, you get a weak sound. You can make the sound stronger by turning up the volume control—increasing the amplification—up to a limit.

The limit is something called *noise.* It's a hissing, sputtering and crackling sound, coming from all kinds of electrical sources: refrigerators, air conditioners, toasters, automobile spark plugs—*even the radio amplifier itself!* On television, these noise sources show up as white streaks and spots called *snow.*

Ordinarily these unwelcome noisemakers don't bother us, because the regular radio and TV waves are much stronger. But consider the waves from a transmitter on the moon or Mars, or from a satellite in orbit around the earth. By the time those waves reach our receivers, they are a trillion times weaker than when they began. To make a clear sound or a clear picture, they need to be amplified enormously.

How do we do this without amplifying the noise equally enormously? In two ways: (1) Shield the receiver so as to keep out all *external* noise. (2) Use an amplifier that doesn't make *internal* noise.

A maser or laser is almost totally free of internal noise. This diagram represents the waves coming out of a maser. These are very high frequency waves. For example,

an ammonia maser's waves have a frequency of about 23,870,000,000 cycles per second. The waves are powerful, free of noise and they carry no information yet.

Here comes the information. These are very feeble radio waves from a temperature-measuring device on Mars. The waves are much too weak to be detected by a

radio receiver. However, they are directed into a maser. They cause the powerful oscillations of the maser to be controlled, shaped and *modulated.* Now the maser's powerful waves are carrying the temperature information "on

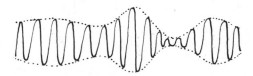

top of" their own, like this. We get tremendous amplification without noise.

The first maser was a bulky affair, with its oven, separator, resonant cavity, wave guide and accessories. Modern masers and lasers are much more compact and efficient. Let's look at a few examples.

The Helium-Neon Laser

Here it is, the whole thing, small enough to hold in your hand. Plug it into an electric socket and it delivers a laser beam more powerful than an early ammonia maser's beam, with much less trouble and at much lower cost.

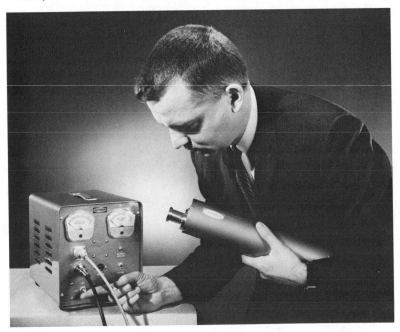

Inside the "wand" of the laser is a glass tube filled with a mixture of two gases: helium and neon. The helium atoms are pumped to higher energy levels (excited) by a high-voltage electric current from the power supply box. That's Step (1). Then,

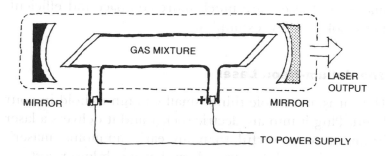

(2) The excited helium atoms collide with neon atoms and pump *them* to their top energy level. The helium atoms, having given up their energy, are now in ground state.

(3) The excited neon atoms, by a chain of stimulated emissions, drop to ground state. During this process they give up their energy, in the form of photons. This step is the basic laser action.

(4) The photons race around inside the tube in all directions, at the speed of light (because they *are* light). Most of the photons are moving from left to right or right to left.

(5) Either way the photons pass through the slanted ends of the tube. (The slant helps to "clear up" reflections in the beam. The effect is somewhat like the way a slanted store window clears up reflections.) The photons strike a curved mirror at either end.

(6) The mirror reflects the photons back into the tube.

They keep going until they strike the other mirror. Back and forth, back and forth, they increase in number by stimulated emission.

(7) At the same time, the photons are being put into phase by the resonance of the tube; the seashell effect.

(8) Very soon, the beam of coherent photons is powerful enough to ram right through the mirror at the right. This mirror is specially constructed; it has only a thin coat of reflective material on it.

(9) A powerful beam of photons can get through and keep going—straight, coherent, controlled and ready to do a job. (Which job? Next chapter.)

The Carbon Dioxide Laser

Here's an example of a more powerful gas laser—the carbon dioxide type. Like the helium-neon laser, it consists of a glass tube filled with gas, and a power supply box to provide high-voltage electric current. It's more powerful for this reason: Carbon dioxide consists of *molecules,* while helium and neon are *atoms.* Let's see why that makes a difference.

Atoms can be excited to high energy levels by forcing electrons away from the nucleus. As they return, they emit photons. That's true for molecules too, because molecules consist of atoms. *But* molecules can also be excited in other ways. For example, let's consider carbon dioxide, CO_2. A molecule of CO_2 is made of one atom of carbon and two atoms of oxygen.

Such a molecule has several possible ways (called modes) of motion:

(1) The oxygen atoms can vibrate to and fro, in a balanced movement toward and away from the carbon atom.

(2) The atoms can vibrate past each other, somewhat like the pyramid effect in the ammonia molecule.

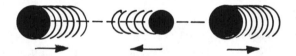

(3) The carbon atom can vibrate left and right.

Each of these modes of vibration contains a certain level of energy. Each of these levels can be stimulated to release its energy, somewhat like the stimulation of an excited atom. So a CO_2 molecule is quite a storehouse of energy, with its three vibrational modes, plus its several electron orbit modes, plus another mode that hasn't been mentioned yet: spin.

Electrons spin like a top while they orbit around the nucleus. The nucleus, too, has a spin of its own and so does the whole CO_2 molecule. All those spins, plus all those vibrational modes, add up to lots of modes in which energy can be stored.

Each mode within a molecule has its own frequency. And different kinds of molecules have different frequencies. The result is a rich choice for the scientists who design lasers, and for the scientists and engineers who use them.

The three lasers we have examined thus far use gases—ammonia, helium-neon and carbon dioxide. There are also liquid lasers and those that use solids. Two of the solid types, the ruby laser and the semi-conductor, are especially interesting. One is quite high-powered and the other is quite small.

The Ruby Laser

Ruby lasers use, as their lasing material, not surprisingly, a ruby. This is a precious stone—not the kind found in mines and used in jewelry—but an artificial ruby crystal, which is grown in the laboratory.

(You can observe the crystal-growing process with salt or sugar. Stir as much as will dissolve in a cupful of warm water. As in the illustration, hang a paper clip on a thread and let it stand for a few days.)

One reason why artifical rubies are used is that they are

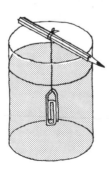

cheaper than natural ones. More importantly, their chemical composition can be exactly controlled. Rubies are composed of a compound, aluminum oxide, with a small amount of chromium atoms distributed within.

The chromium atoms deliver the laser action. They are pumped to the excited state by a flash lamp, quite similar to the flash lamps used in photography. In one form of ruby laser, designed by Dr. Theodore Maiman in 1960, the flash lamp was coiled around a rod-shaped ruby. In another form, the flash lamp was straight and lay parallel to the ruby rod.

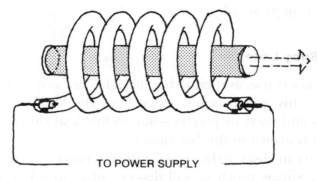

TO POWER SUPPLY

The pumping action of the flash lamp produces the same three steps as in the gas lasers:

(1) *Population inversion.* Photons from the flash lamp strike the chromium atoms and pump them to their excited state.

(2) *Spontaneous emission.* Some excited chromium atoms emit photons (as they drop to lower energy levels).

(3) *Stimulated emission.* These emitted photons strike other excited chromium atoms. Each atom is stimulated to emit a second photon,

coherent with the first. A swift doubling and redoubling takes place inside the ruby.

The pairs of photons streak back and forth through the length of the ruby. At each end they are reflected by the mirrored ends of the ruby. They are joined by more pairs of photons. The ruby is exactly the right length for the photons' waves to be put into resonance. When the photons have piled up to sufficient strength, they burst through the partially silvered mirror at the right. They keep going, in a straight, coherent and controlled beam.

The first dramatic use of lasers was done with a ruby laser. The beam punched a hole in a razor blade. While this was merely a stunt, you can guess some other useful applications, such as drilling and cutting hard materials.

A ruby laser made the front-page headlines in 1960. A thin beam of ruby laser light, about the thickness of a pencil, was aimed at the moon. It was reflected by the moon's rocky surface and detected by a light meter on earth.

This feat is possible because the coherent light of the laser emerges straight and narrow. In its 800,000-kilometer round trip, earth to moon and back, it spreads out very little. So it stays "packed" and can be detected. But the incoherent light from the most powerful searchlight would spread and "thin out" so much that it would be impossible to detect after such a long trip.

The Semi-conductor Laser

This is the kind of instrument that should excite the writers of science fiction. Its main working part is a crystal about 1 millimeter long. (This dash—is about 3 millimeters in length.) Here's the semi-conductor crystal, enlarged twenty times.

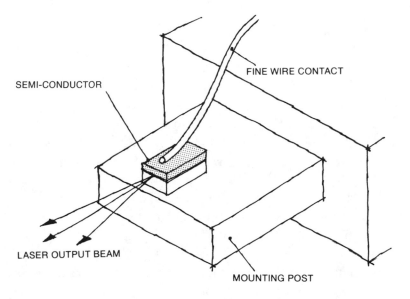

What can you do with a source of strong, coherent light that can be carried in a coat pocket? To help you speculate, let's look at a semi-conductor laser in more detail.

First, let's look at its name. A semi-conductor is a substance that is classed between the good conductors of electricity and the non-conductors. The good conductors are mainly metals such as copper, aluminum, silver, gold, iron and so forth. The non-conductors (insulators) are mainly non-metals such as glass, rubber, porcelain, wood, cloth and most plastics. Most semi-conductors are certain metals such as silicon, selenium, gallium or compounds of these metals. Semi-conductors are used in transistor radios and in photo light meters.

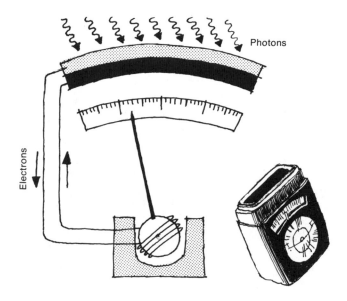

The semi-conductor in a light meter is like a laser in reverse. Light—a stream of photons—shines on the semi-conductor. The photons push electrons in the semi-conductor up to the excited state. They are pushed up *and out*, into an electric meter and back into the semi-conductor. This stream of electrons is an electric current. The amount of current is shown on the electric meter. The brighter the light, the larger the current.

So, in the semi-conductor of a light meter, *photons come in*, and *electrons flow out*. On a larger scale, this principle is used for generating electric current for space vehicles of various kinds (see page 76). The "solar panels" of a space vehicle are large flat plates made of semi-conductor materials. *Photons* of sunlight *come into* the panels; an *electric current flows out* of the panels (into the instruments and electrical machines of the space vehicle).

The reverse action takes place in a semi-conductor laser. An *electric current flows into* the semi-conductor, and *photons* of coherent light *come out*. Here it is, step by step:

(1) An electric current, from a battery or other source, flows into the semi-conductor, a crystal of gallium arsenide.

(2) The current pumps electrons into the excited state. This causes a population inversion—more excited atoms than ground-state atoms.

(3) Then comes the three steps that take place in all lasers: (a) excited atoms emit photons by spontaneous emission; (b) these photons strike other excited atoms, and pairs of photons are produced by stimulated emission; (c) pair after pair, a supply of photons is built up by stimulated emission.

These photon pairs are reflected back and forth by the polished ends of the crystal, as in the ruby laser. They are put into phase by resonance and discharged through one end. They are sent out to work, as described in the next chapter.

And there are still other lasers, of different powers and sizes, able to do different jobs. There are lasers that can drill 10,000 separate holes along this line_____. There are lasers that can send 2,000 separate telephone messages at the same time through a glass fiber as thin as a hair. There are lasers . . .

Before we look at more lasers, let's look again at the *qualities* of laser light that enable all these things to happen.

Special Qualities of Laser Light

(1) LASER LIGHT IS INTENSE

Think of a cluster of seventy 100-watt bulbs shining at you. Quite a bright light. Now imagine *all* that light shining out

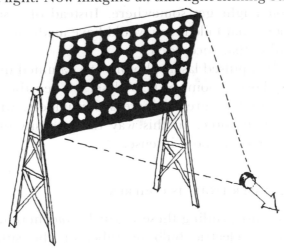

of *one* small lamp—one square centimeter in area. That's *really* bright . . . in fact, it's the brightness of *one square centimeter* of the sun's surface. Scientists have measured the sun's light output. It is 7,000 watts, or *7 kilowatts*, per square centimeter.

Now, the light output of a laser. A high-powered laser, focused to a point, can deliver at that point the brightness of *one billion kilowatts* per square centimeter!

Of course that's a special high-powered laser. And it can't deliver a *steady* stream of high-powered laser light. (A steady stream is called continuous wave, or C.W.) It's a *pulsed* laser, and that word needs an explanation.

Suppose you pick up a one-pound hammer and deliver a steady stream of wallops, one per second, on a layer of soft gravel. Result: a layer of crushed gravel.

Now try the same hammering on a hard granite boulder. Result: no change. The boulder is too hard to be broken by a stream of one-pound blows.

Suppose you could *store up* the energy needed for a hundred blows, then pick up a 100-pound hammer. Then you might get somewhere. Instead of a stream of little blows that failed, you would have made one giant blow, or pulse, that succeeded.

In a pulsed laser, photons are dammed up, way past the "spillover" point of C.W. lasers. Then they are suddenly released in greatly increased numbers, with greatly increased force. In this way the intensity of laser light is made even more intense.

(2) LASER LIGHT IS COHERENT

You are reading these words by *in*coherent light emitted by an electric bulb or tube, or the sun or a flame.

Incoherent light is a jumble of frequencies and wavelengths. *Coherent* light—from one wave to the next and the next, the waves are equally *spaced.* Equally spaced waves are said to be *spatially coherent.* The spatial coherence of laser light makes it useful in all kinds of spatial measurement, from the diameter of bacteria to the diameter of Mars.

The number of waves per second (frequency) of laser light is constant, second after second. Waves that are equal in *time* are said to be *temporally* coherent. The temporal coherence of laser light makes it useful in the accurate timing of all kinds of events—even those that happen in a hundred-billionth of a second.

(3) LASER LIGHT IS MONOCHROMATIC

It contains only one single color. Put a colored slide in an ordinary projector, turn on the light and focus the image on a screen. The picture is *almost,* but not exactly, sharp. A truly sharp picture is impossible because the lens cannot focus all colors of light equally well. If you focus for the blue parts of the picture, the reds and greens are slightly out of focus. Focus for red, and the greens and blues are slightly out. But laser light is entirely of one color— monochromatic. So a lens can focus it to an absolutely sharp point. Later you will see how that makes it possible to do painless surgery inside a living eye and to drill tiny holes in the hardest substance.

(4) LASER LIGHT IS DIRECTIONAL

Ordinary incoherent light is not. Shine an ordinary flashlight out at the sky on a dark night and you will see the beam spread out and disappear. Shine a laser light and it goes on and on and on. A pencil-thick red beam from a ruby laser was aimed at the moon. In its 400,000-kilometer trip to the moon, it had spread out to a circle only two kilometers in diameter. And most of that spread was caused by the earth's atmosphere. In empty space the beam would have spread only a few meters.

The directional quality of laser light makes it especially useful to surveyors. They use lasers for laying out straight lines and measuring distances, especially in difficult places. More about that later.

Laser light is: Intense
Spatially coherent
Temporally coherent
Monochromatic
Directional

Let's see how these qualities of laser light are put to work.

LASERS AT WORK

Lasers for Healing

Look at these before-and-after pictures.

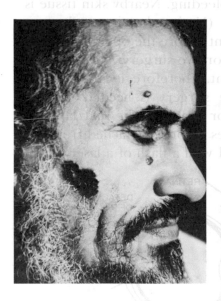

Those dark spots and areas are skin tumors. Not only are they ugly, they are also dangerous. They can grow larger, pieces can loosen and enter the blood stream beneath the skin, travel to other parts of the body and start other tumors.

Skin tumors can be removed surgically by cutting with a knife. Now a new method, laser surgery, has been developed. These photographs show the results of an operation with a laser beam as the surgical instrument.

The intense energy of the laser beam is focused to a very sharp point. When this point is aimed at skin tissue, it causes a quick heating-up. The temperature is high enough to change water in the tissue to water vapor. The solid material is burned away in puffs of smoke.

The beam is moved up and down and across the tumor. Painlessly, a tiny bit at a time, the tumor is vaporized and burned away. Blood vessels near the tumor are sealed off by the heat, so there is no bleeding. Nearby skin tissue is not affected by the beam. (Notice that it wasn't even necessary to shave the patient before the operation.)

Another use of lasers is for eye surgery. A laser beam can be focused to a fine point. Therefore, it can be aimed exactly at the place where surgery is needed without disturbing nearby tissue. For example, the rear layer of the eye, the retina, sometimes becomes detached from the eyeball. It can be reattached with a flash of a laser beam.

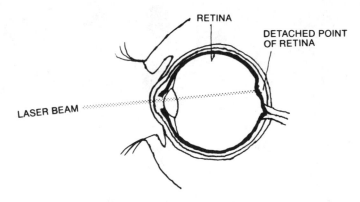

This causes a pinpoint area of the retina to heat up, just enough to "weld" the retina to the eyeball surface. Many tiny welds are made, at different parts of the retina.

This laser welding process causes a high temperature at each spot on the retina. Then why doesn't the laser beam, as it passes through, damage the interior of the eye? There are two reasons:

(1) The interior of the eye is transparent. The laser beam shines right through without affecting it. You can see a similar effect with two clear bottles or tumblers. Fill one with clear water and the other with dark-colored water (coffee or tea, for example). Let both stand in the sunlight and compare their temperature.

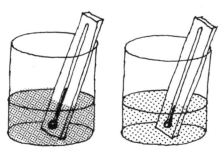

(2) The laser beam is cone-shaped. At the base of the cone the laser energy is spread over a large area. Each small portion of the area receives a small portion of the energy. But the point of the cone receives all of the energy of the laser beam, in a very small area.

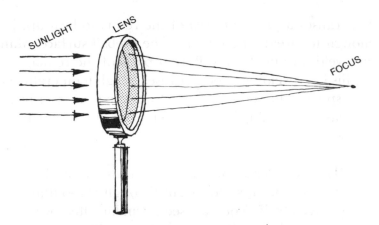

You can observe the effect with a magnifying glass. (Magnifying lenses are sometimes called burning glasses).

Hold the lens in sunlight over a small piece of black paper in a dish or pie pan. Hold it at such a distance that it casts a circle of light on the paper. After half a minute, touch the paper. It may have warmed up only very slightly. The energy of sunlight, passing through the lens, was spread over the whole circular area.

Now move the lens to form a small point of light. All the light energy through the lens is being focused on a very small spot of paper. Notice how bright the spot is. Watch the paper begin to smoke, or perhaps even catch fire. (That's why you need a dish.)

Surgical lasers, then, can be used as tiny torches for tumor surgery or as tiny spot welders for eye surgery. A third use is as surgical knives. The thin, fine laser beam can cut a fine controlled line through skin and muscle tissue, sharp as a knife. Unlike a knife, there is almost no bleeding, because the heat seals off the blood vessels as they are cut.

Another valuable surgical laser uses *fiber optics*. A pencil-thick flexible cable is made of hundreds of glass fibers side by side. The fibers conduct laser light without "spilling" any of it sideways. The cable can be passed through the mouth into the stomach. A laser beam is sent through the cable. The beam can work as a knife, to cut

out tumors, or as a welder to seal off bleeding blood vessels. The cable is not exactly comfortable for the patient, but it is much easier for the surgeon and the patient than cutting open the abdomen.

There are many other medical and surgical uses of lasers, and more are being invented. One of the recent ones: to remove tattoos from people who have changed their minds about owning them. While that may not be your problem, you will surely welcome another experimental use of lasers: to drill out tooth cavities without the use of a drill—and without pain!

Lasers in the Factory

Stroll through a factory—any factory—and you can find dozens of possible uses for lasers. Most of these possibilities are related to the *controlled intensity* of laser light. Lasers can cut, weld, drill, melt and vaporize any substance.

Of course you can do most of those jobs with ordinary tools: knives, torches, drills, furnaces and so forth. And that's how they are ordinarily done. But look at some special jobs that lasers do especially well.

CUTTING HARD-SURFACED MATERIALS

Some machine parts need to have very hard surfaces. But hard-surfaced objects are sometimes brittle. Cut them with a blade, or drill them with a drill, and they may crack apart from the vibration and from the heat of friction. There is no vibration with a laser beam, just very high heat for a fraction of a second on a very small area.

The most spectacular example of such work is drilling holes in diamonds. Diamonds are extremely hard, through and through. Cheaper grades of diamonds are used in making thin copper wire. A hole is drilled in the diamond and copper is forced through. These holes used to be made by drilling through the diamond with diamond dust. To drill one hole took about two *days* of constant drilling—and sometimes the diamond suddenly shattered from the vibration. Nowadays, thanks to laser beams the hole is drilled, without vibration, in two *minutes*.

WELDING DIFFICULT MATERIALS

Watch a welding job being done in a machine shop or auto repair garage. It looks clumsy and it is. It is suitable for joining together large pieces of metal. But for precision work, on tiny pieces or finely shaped objects, it is not so good.

This is where the laser, with its tiny high-intensity beam, is much better. It can weld the hair-thin wire from a semi-conductor crystal to its metal support, without heating the crystal. It can weld metals that have very high melting points, without heating nearby areas. It can weld two different metals that will not join at usual welding temperatures. And the job is done much quicker, so that the metal is less weakened by heating.

CUTTING AT HIGH SPEED

A pulsed laser beam works so quickly that it can burn off bits of metal from a rapidly spinning wheel. A sensing mechanism feels where the wheel is out of balance. The mechanism sends a message to the laser, which sends a pulse of light to the heavy spot on the wheel. Pulse after pulse, a few molecules at a time, the whirling wheel is trimmed into perfect balance.

The high cutting speed of lasers is useful in garment factories. Cloth is laid out on a table. A laser beam, guided by a computer, makes a fine cut, thin as a thread, through the cloth. All the pieces for an entire suit are cut in less than two minutes.

Lasers for Holography

With a slide projector and a picture slide, you can project a flat (two-dimensional) picture on a screen. The picture is the same no matter where you stand (as long as you are in front of the screen). If the picture is a front view portrait, it remains a front view. Whether you're directly in front of

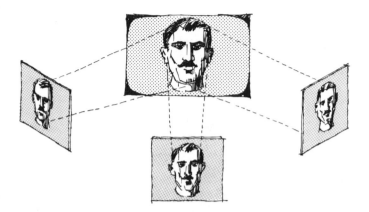

the screen or to the left or right you see a front view. The same is true for a television picture.

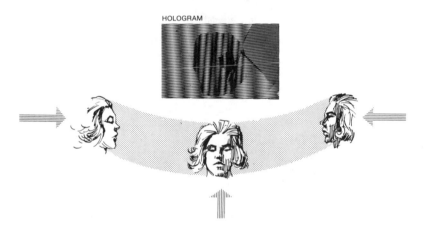

Now imagine a picture that *changes* as you change position! From the front you see a front view. From the left side you see a left view. From the right side you see a right view. Such a picture is a three-dimensional picture, a

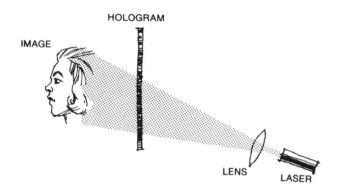

whole picture, called a *hologram*. (The *w* got lost somewhere along the way.)

In some ways a hologram is like the sound coming out of a record player. Let's explore that idea:

This wiggly line is a diagram of sound waves from a deep-voiced cello recorded on a phonograph record.

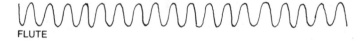

This line shows sound waves from a high-pitched flute.

When both instruments play at the same time, their combined waves are recorded like this.

Play the record, and the single line is heard as two different sounds. Your ears and your brain are able to recognize two instruments in the one wiggly line.

Now we come to holography, which was invented in 1947 by Dennis Gabor, a British scientist. At the time there were no lasers, and holography was done with incoherent light. The use of laser light has vastly improved the process.

The diagram shows a laser emitting a beam of coherent laser light. The beam strikes a partly silvered mirror called a *beam splitter*. Part of the light is *transmitted* through this mirror. It is then reflected by another mirror through a lens onto a photographic film. This beam is called the *reference beam*.

The other part of the beam is *reflected* by the beam

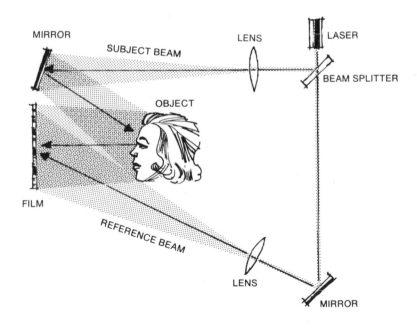

splitter. This part is called the *subject beam*. It is reflected by a mirror onto the subject being photographed. The subject reflects the beam onto the same photographic film.

So the film has received both portions of the original coherent laser beam. One portion, the reference beam, came unchanged from the laser lamp. The other half, the subject beam, was reflected from the subject before reaching the film. The two halves started out as entirely coherent. But they are no longer coherent when they reach the film.

On some parts of the film two waves may arrive like this, producing a double-strength wave. This is called a *reinforcement*.

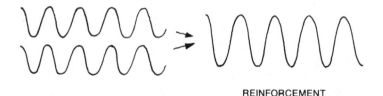

REINFORCEMENT

On other parts of the film they may arrive like this, producing a *cancellation*.

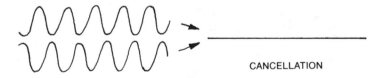

CANCELLATION

When the film is developed, it shows a record of the reinforcements and cancellations. There's no image on it, just a puzzling set of dark and light fringes. But when the film is illuminated by laser light, it produces a three-dimensional image in space! Your eyes and brain are able to recognize the image produced by the set of fringes.

What practical uses can we figure out for holography? As a starter, think of high speed three-dimensional photography. For example, here's the crank-shaft of a newly designed automobile engine. When it whirls at eighty revolutions per second, how does the shape of the crank-shaft change? Does it bend anywhere? Does it need to be stiffened at those places? Does the bend change as the speed increases or decreases? A series of holograms, taken with high-speed flashes of laser light, gives the answer. Can you suggest some other industrial or scientific uses?

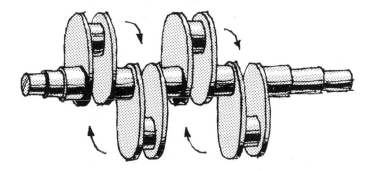

Holographic movies are just as feasible. Someday you may see actors right in front of you, large as life, in color, seemingly real—except that you can walk right through them. What an opportunity for writers of science fiction or murder mysteries!

Measuring with Lasers

Scientists, physicians, engineers and manufacturers— people who work with matter, energy, time and space— need to make measurements of all kinds. *How far* is it to the moon? *How large* is the nucleus of a nerve cell? *How many* vibrations per second are there in that machine? *How much* does the bridge cable stretch under full load? Often such questions can be answered by means of instruments using lasers. Here are some examples:

How wide is that river? Set up a low-powered laser on one bank of the river. Set up a reflector (a mirror on a stand) on the other bank. The laser beam travels across the river and is reflected back to an instrument next to the laser. A timer in the instrument measures the time interval for the round trip. A computer converts this time interval into distance. (Light travels almost exactly 300,000 kilometers per second, or 3 kilometers in a hundred-thousandth of a second.)

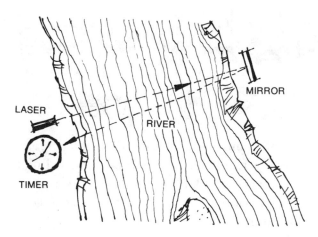

How high is a certain mountain on the moon? With a laser, timer and computer, measure the distance from earth to the base of the mountain, and then to the peak. The height can be calculated from these figures.

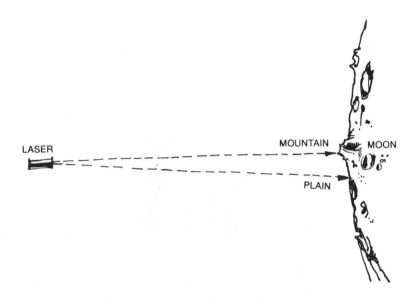

How can we mark off a perfectly straight line 10 kilometers long to guide a machine for boring a tunnel? Set up a low-powered ruby laser and be guided by it. Its pencil-thin red beam will shine perfectly straight, narrow and visible for the boring machine to follow.

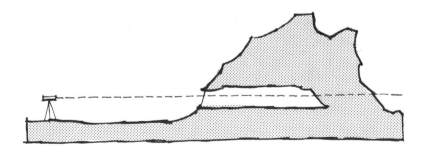

How much does a box of oatmeal cost? In many super-markets the answer is supplied by an electronic checkout machine. A checkout clerk holds the oatmeal box over a scanner. Out of the scanner comes a low-power laser beam. The beam vibrates back and forth across a pattern of lines and spaces on the box. Some lines and spaces are thick, some are medium, some are thin.

The vibrating laser beam is reflected by the lines and spaces. Black lines are poor reflectors. White spaces are good reflectors. A photoelectric cell (electric eye) receives the reflections and changes them into electric pulses, like dots and dashes. These go into a computer (decoding

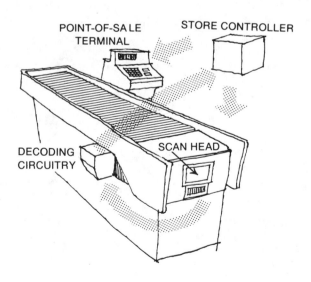

circuitry) that "recognizes" the dot-dash patterns. The computer then sends a price signal into the cash register (point-of-sale terminal).

For example, the pattern of lines and spaces on page 96 contains the following information:

A. The two thin lines on the left, with a narrow white space between, are the signal for "This is as far as the pattern goes on this side." Find the same signal at the right side of the pattern.

B. The cluster of lines and spaces from the left to the middle is the code for "Quaker Oats Company."

C. The cluster of lines and spaces from the middle to the right is the code for "Instant Oatmeal, Regular Flavor, 10-ounce box."

So the box has been identified by maker, contents and weight, in about a nanosecond. The computer searches through its electronic memory (in another nanosecond) and finds that this item costs eighty-nine cents today. (The memory can be easily changed as prices change.) The computer sends this information to the cash register, which rings up eighty-nine cents.

The whole system's operation is based on the coherence of laser light. Such light can be focused to a tiny, sharp narrow beam. It can pick out lines and spaces swiftly and accurately, thousands per second. The checkout clerk doesn't even have to hold the box still, but just wave it across the scan head. This system is much faster, more accurate, and much easier on the checkout clerk than looking for price stamps and punching cash register keys.

How quickly is the ship (or submarine or airplane) changing direction? A laser gyro in the pilot room (top of page 98) tells the answer. The instrument is mounted in a horizontal position. The laser emits *two* beams, to the left

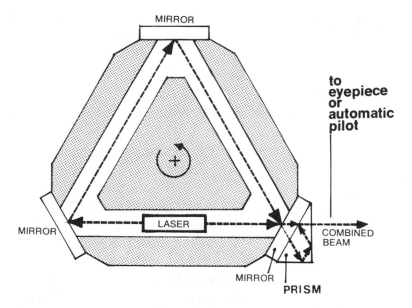

and right. The right beam goes out straight to the right.
The left beam is reflected by mirrors: it goes in a triangu-
lar course and meets the right beam.

All the parts of the instrument are adjusted so that the
two beams meet in phase. The combined beam is seen as a
bright line. (All this is done while the ship is stationary.)

When the ship is moving straight ahead, the two beams
continue to meet in phase. The combined beam continues
to show as a bright line.

But if the ship starts to turn (a wind or current may
cause it) the beams are thrown out of phase. Instead of a
bright line, there are dark and light bands—interference
fringes—moving to the left or right. The faster the turn,
the faster the fringes move.

The pilot observes these and corrects his course. Or the
gyro instrument can be connected to an automatic pilot
that controls the steering machinery.

Why does the turning of the ship throw the beams out of phase? Here's a way to think about it. This is *not* an explanation but a sort of comparison:

Suppose you can walk *up* a stationary escalator in 30 seconds. But if the escalator is also moving *upward*, you can do it in less time. If the escalator is moving *downward*, you will need more time.

Interferometers

Several other measuring instruments work by interference patterns. Such instruments are called *interferometers*. Let's look at the way they make measurements.

Hold both hands, fingers outstretched, against the sky or a light. You can see light areas (the sky or light) and dark areas (your fingers). Then place one hand over the other, so that the fingers of one hand fit in the spaces of the other hand. Now you can't see light, because the fingers of one hand interfere with the light in the spaces of the other hand.

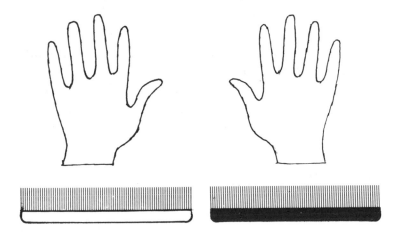

Next, slide one hand to the left, for the width of one finger. At the moment of sliding over, you will see a flash of light; then darkness as the fingers of one hand interfere with the light in the spaces of the other.

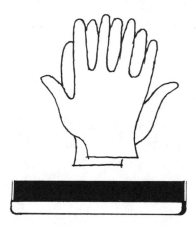

Try again, for the width of two fingers: two flashes. Three fingers: three flashes. If you know the width of your fingers, you would know how far you had moved them, just by counting the flashes.

Try it again, with two combs of the same size. The teeth are closer together than your fingers, so one flash is a smaller measurement. Let's use the combs as an interferometer in order to measure the diameter of a coin.

Count the number of teeth per centimeter. Place the combs one over the other, matching the ends, light coming through. Place the edge of the coin against the right edge of the top comb. Slide the coin to the left so that it pushes the comb to the left. Count the light flashes as you do so, until the coin has moved all the way in, as shown.

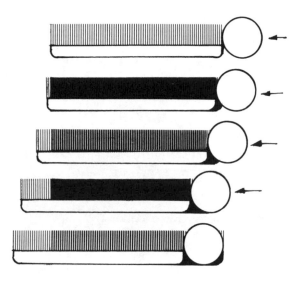

Suppose your combs have ten teeth per centimeter. Suppose you counted twenty flashes as you moved the coin. Then your coin is 2 centimeters in diameter. You didn't have to look at lines and numbers on a ruler. You just had to count flashes. If your combs had twenty teeth per centimeter your results would be twice as accurate. Still more teeth per centimeter, still more accurate. But there's a limit to the number of teeth on a comb.

The limit on light waves is much higher. For instance, in the light from a helium-neon laser, there are 63,280 waves in the space of one centimeter. Suppose we have two beams of helium-neon light as our two "combs." When the beams are matched, wave to wave, in phase, we see brightness. When we slide one of the beams, the waves are out of phase; we see cancellations, dark lines produced by interference. Keep sliding the beam, light and blackout, light and blackout. This is like sliding the coin that pushed the comb. The "coin" itself is the object being measured— a plastic film one molecule thick, for example, or a blood corpuscle, or a grain of dust.

It doesn't take long to count twenty flashes in the comb experiment. It would take you much longer to count several hundred flashes to measure the thickness of a sheet of cellophane. But you don't have to; an electronic counter does the job in less than a second.

Laser Light for Communication

In his right hand, the boy holds a telephone cable used fifty years ago. There are 2,000 pairs of wires in it. The

cable could conduct 2,000 separate conversations at a time, by means of electric currents.

In his left hand he holds a glass fiber, almost as thin as a hair. It too can conduct 2,000 separate conversations at a time, by means of laser light.

The first telephone lines, one hundred years ago, carried one message in one pair of wires. Then a method was developed for feeding several messages into one pair of wires, without mixing them up. At the other end they were selected out, separated, by filter devices. These are similar to the tuner of your radio, or the channel selector of your TV, which can select one program out of the many being broadcast.

Sending several messages through one pair of wires is called *multiplexing,* from the Latin for "many-folding." Multiplexing saves space, materials, labor and money.

However, there's a limit to the number of messages that can be sent through one pair of wires at the same time. The limit is set mainly by a condition called *thermal noise.* This is a kind of agitation, a shaking of electrons in the wires. This produces a faint sizzling and sputtering sound. Electric currents in the wire increase the thermal noise.

Thermal noise is usually not loud enough to matter. But when multiplexing is overdone, with too many currents adding to the general thermal noise, the unwanted sound becomes a bother.

There's no thermal noise with laser light. A laser beam is pure coherent *light*—photons—with no electrons to shake up. So thousands of messages can be carried by laser light in a single glass fiber. Each message is filtered out at the far end.

The first large-scale experimental use of this method

was begun in Chicago, in 1976, and in Brussels, Belgium, in 1978. Telephone companies expect it to be widespread within a few years. There will be enormous savings in materials, labor and under-street space when glass fibers replace copper cables, and laser light replaces electric current.

Some problems had been solved before the Chicago experiment was begun:

> (1) How to keep laser light from "leaking" out of a glass fiber, across into a neighboring fiber. This isn't a problem when the fibers are straight. The directionality of laser light makes it stay straight in a straight conductor. But around a bend, some of the light leaks out. After passing through a few dozen bends the light is almost gone.
>
> The problem was solved by coating the glass fibers with a different kind of glass. This coating, called *cladding*, acts as a kind

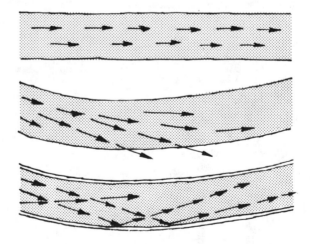

of reflector. The laser light stays in the cladded fiber.

(2) How to get laser *light* to carry a message that began as *sound*. This is done by means of the *carrier wave* system.

This is a graph of a laser beam, when nobody is speaking.

And this is a graph of sound waves in air, made by someone speaking into a telephone.

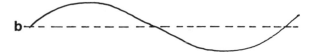

The sound waves alter, or *modulate*, the carrier waves, which now look like this.

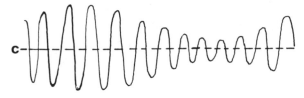

The modulated light waves are conducted through glass fibers, mile after mile under the streets of the city. At the other end we come to the next problem that had to be solved:

(3) How to change light waves into sound waves. This was done in two steps: (a) changing light waves into electrical vibrations and (b) changing electrical vibrations into sound waves.

Job (a) is done by a device that works like a photographic light meter. It *receives* light waves and gives out vibrations of electric currents. Job (b) is done by your telephone receiver. It receives electric vibrations and gives out sound waves.

Transducers

Jobs (a) and (b) are done by instruments that receive one form of energy and give out another. Such instruments are called *transducers* (from the Latin for "lead across"). Scientific laboratories are full of transducers, and your home contains a fair number too.

For instance, your telephone *transmitter* receives sound waves and gives out electrical vibrations. A doorbell receives electric current and gives out sound waves. A radio receiver receives radio waves and gives out sound waves. A TV set receives radio waves and gives out light waves and sound waves. An electric toaster receives electric current and gives out heat (and some light).

It's an interesting way to observe the gadgets and instruments around you. What form of energy goes in? What form of energy is given out?

Lasers in the Laboratory

Test tubes, Bunsen burners, microscopes and balances— these are standard items in every scientific laboratory.

Now, for many laboratories, we can add another—lasers.

Lasers are powerful tools for scientists, mainly because of the *selective* ability of laser light. This can be compared to the selective ability of the pendulum setup described earlier. Here it is again, with some changes.

Pendulum *A* is the same length as pendulum *C*. If *A* is set swinging, *C* will swing along, resonating to the frequency of *A*. Change the length (and therefore the frequency) of *A* to be the same as *E*, and that one will resonate. You can *select* any pendulum to resonate by setting pendulum *A* to the frequency of that pendulum.

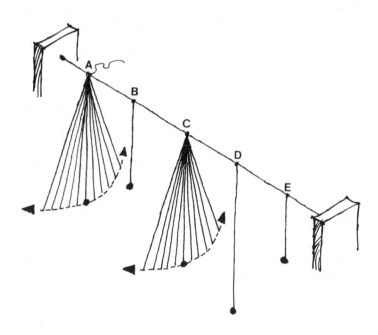

Selection can be done with lasers. First, there are many different kinds of lasing materials. Each emits its own frequency or group of frequencies. Second, there are

tunable lasers, whose frequency can be adjusted—
tuned—within a certain range.

And there is another kind of laser selection available to
scientists—power. Clearing up a blood clot in the eye
requires very little power. Melting a hard steel alloy
requires a great deal. There are lasers for each use. Let's
look at some of the laser jobs done by scientists.

(1) *A chemist* is studying smog caused by nitrogen
dioxide (NO_2) in automobile exhaust. There are many
other substances in the exhaust—oxygen, nitrogen, sulfur
dioxide and dozens of others. Question: How does a
hot-day rise in temperature affect the behavior of the NO_2
alone? Set the laser to emit the frequency of the NO_2
molecules in the exhaust gas. These molecules will begin to
resonate, to vibrate and to heat up. Other molecules are
unaffected.

(2) *A biologist* wants to isolate and examine cancerous
bone-marrow cells. There may be one cancerous cell to
100 normal ones. Formerly, batches of marrow cells were
stained with a dye, placed on microscope slides and
examined one after the other, to find the cancerous cells.
Now, the marrow cells, in a liquid, flow in a thin glass tube
through which a laser beam is shining. The laser light has
a frequency that causes certain materials in cancerous cells
to resonate and glow. A machine responds to this glow,
and separates these cells from the normal ones, at the rate
of 50,000 cells per *minute!*

(3) *A surgeon* wants to destroy a blood clot inside the eye
of a person who has been in an auto accident. Normally,
blood clots are absorbed in a few days. But this one is
persistent and may cause partial blindness. The surgeon
shines a pinpoint beam of green laser light on the clot. The
red clot absorbs green light and transforms it to heat. The

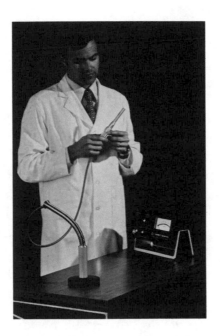

clot is vaporized and burned away, without affecting eye tissue only a hundredth of a millimeter away.

(The same kind of selection works for the balloon-within-a-balloon stunt, shown on page 2. The outside balloon is transparent; it transmits light. The inside balloon is black; it transforms the light into heat and the balloon pops.)

(4) *A physicist* is experimenting on nuclear fusion. This is the process for obtaining enormous amounts of energy from special forms of hydrogen called deuterium and tritium. These atomic fuels can be obtained from seawater. A gallon of seawater will give the energy of 300 gallons of gasoline.

Extracting the fuels is not too difficult a process. The difficulty is in forcing them to combine and release energy. A very high temperature, about 100 million degrees C., is needed. Scientists are experimenting with pulsed high-power laser beams, focused on tiny pellets containing the fuel. The experiments look promising.

All over the world thousands and thousands of lasers are in use in research laboratories. Most of them are serving useful purposes: promoting health, improving manufacturing processes and probing deeper into the laws of science.

But some lasers are being used for research on destruction. The laser that can drill a hole in a diamond in two minutes can blind a person in one second. The laser beam that guides a drill in a tunnel can guide a bomb to its target. The tunable laser that can destroy a tumor can be tuned to produce a tumor. Today, giant pulses of laser light can weld huge steel girders together. Someday, if the research is "successful," giant pulses of laser light from airplanes may set fire to homes miles below.

Lasers cannot choose their work. Only people can.

INDEX